THE
MILITARY HISTORY
QUIZ BOOK

OSPREY

THE
OSPREY
QUIZMASTER

First published in Great Britain in 2010 by Osprey Publishing,
Midland House, West Way, Botley, Oxford, OX2 0PH, UK
44-02 23rd Street, Suite 205A, Long Island City, NY 11101, USA

E-mail: info@ospreypublishing.com

© 2010 Osprey Publishing Ltd.

A CIP catalog record for this book is available from the British Library

ISBN: 978 1 84908 172 6

Page layout by Myriam Bell Design, France
Typeset in Bembo and Aachen
Cover originated by PDQ Media, Bungay, UK
Printed in China through Worldprint Ltd

10 11 12 13 14   10 9 8 7 6 5 4 3 2 1

Osprey Publishing is supporting the Woodland Trust, the UK's leading woodland conservation
charity, by funding the dedication of trees.

www.ospreypublishing.com

EASY QUESTIONS

★

ONE-STAR GENERAL KNOWLEDGE

QUIZ 1
GENERAL, MULTIPLE CHOICE

1. The Irish king Brian Boru was killed in which battle?

   ❑ a. Clontarf   ❑ b. Boyne
   ❑ c. Glen Mama   ❑ d. Sulchoid

2. Which day "will live in infamy"?

   ❑ a. May 7, 1915: the sinking of the *Lusitania*
   ❑ b. May 10, 1940: the German invasion of France
   ❑ c. December 7, 1941: The Japanese attack on Pearl Harbor
   ❑ d. August 6, 1945: the dropping of the atomic bomb
      on Hiroshima

3. Which warrior was most likely to use a *pilum*?

   ❑ a. Mongol horseman   ❑ b. Egyptian charioteer
   ❑ c. Japanese samurai   ❑ d. Roman legionary

4. In which year did Horatio Nelson win his famous victory at the battle of the Nile?

   ❑ a. 1792   ❑ b. 1798
   ❑ c. 1804   ❑ d. 1811

5. What was the name given to the North American P-51 fighter?

   ❑ a. Thunderbolt   ❑ b. Lightning
   ❑ c. Mustang   ❑ d. Kittyhawk

6. Who led the Israelites to victory at the battle of Jericho?

   ❑ a. King David   ❑ b. Saul
   ❑ c. Sampson   ❑ d. Joshua

7. What was the birth name of the Mongol warlord Genghis Khan?

☐ a. Temüjin   ☐ b. Timur
☐ c. Ogedei   ☐ d. Yesukhei

8. Which World War I fighter pilot is credited with the most confirmed aerial victories?

☐ a. Charley Brown   ☐ b. Manfred von Richthofen
☐ c. Albert Ball   ☐ d. Eric Hartmann

9. The Exocet missile is named after which animal?

☐ a. bat   ☐ b. flying fish
☐ c. snake   ☐ d. spider

10. Which general led the Union Army at the 1863 battle of Gettysburg?

☐ a. Ulysses S. Grant   ☐ b. Joseph Hooker
☐ c. Ambrose E. Burnside   ☐ d. George Meade

DID YOU KNOW?

George Armstrong Custer's younger brother Thomas won two Medals of Honor in the same week during the American Civil War. In that week, he single-handedly captured two Confederate battle standards, took 14 enemy prisoners, lost two horses, and took a pistol shot through his face. Tom later died fighting alongside his brother at the battle of the Little Bighorn.

QUIZ 2

GENERAL, TRUE OR FALSE

1. Julius Caesar was once captured by pirates, and his friends were forced to pay a ransom for his safe return.
   ❑ True   ❑ False

2. Arthur Wellesley (later Duke of Wellington) and Horatio Nelson never met.
   ❑ True   ❑ False

3. Fewer than 3,000 men died at the battle of the Boyne in 1690.
   ❑ True   ❑ False

4. "Caltrops" are multi-pronged metal spikes spread over the ground, primarily to injure horses.
   ❑ True   ❑ False

5. More Americans died in the Vietnam War than in World War I.
   ❑ True   ❑ False

6. The first Punic War began due to a territorial dispute in Greece.
   ❑ True   ❑ False

7. Audie Murphy, America's most decorated soldier, was turned down by the Marine Corps because of his small stature.
   ❑ True   ❑ False

8. Every year on April 30, the French Foreign Legion salutes a wooden hand.
   ❑ True   ❑ False

9. The radio communication word "Wilco" is short for "will comply."
   ❑ True   ❑ False

10. George Armstrong Custer finished second-to-last in his graduating class at West Point.
    ❑ True   ❑ False

QUIZ 3
AMERICAN CIVIL WAR, MULTIPLE CHOICE

1. After South Carolina, which state was the second to secede from the Union?

   ☐ a. North Carolina   ☐ b. Virginia
   ☐ c. Texas   ☐ d. Mississippi

2. The 1862 battle of Fredericksburg was fought over which river?

   ☐ a. Rappahannock   ☐ b. Cumberland
   ☐ c. Potomac   ☐ d. James

3. Which Confederate general was famous for his use of "foot cavalry"?

   ☐ a. James Longstreet
   ☐ b. Joseph E. Johnston

DID YOU KNOW?

During the bombardment of Fort Sumter, which signaled the start of the American Civil War, Confederate gunners fired more than 4,000 rounds. Despite this intense fire, the Union defenders suffered no casualties and eventually surrendered as much from want of food as from enemy fire. Unfortunately, as the Union soldiers left the fort, they fired off a salute to their flag and one was killed due to an accidental ammunition explosion. Private Daniel Hough thus became the first fatality of the American Civil War.

❑ c. Thomas J. "Stonewall" Jackson
❑ d. Nathan Bedford Forrest

4. In which year did General McClellan face General Johnston in the battle of Fair Oaks?

❑ a. 1861   ❑ b. 1862
❑ c. 1863   ❑ d. 1864

5. Joshua Chamberlain began the Civil War as the lieutenant colonel of which regiment?

❑ a. 20th Maine   ❑ b. 16th Maine
❑ c. 14th Connecticut   ❑ d. 8th Connecticut

6. How many states officially joined the Confederacy?

❑ a. 9   ❑ b. 10
❑ c. 11   ❑ d. 13

7. Which Confederate general gave the order to open fire on Fort Sumter, the first shots of the war?

❑ a. Joseph Johnston   ❑ b. A. P. Hill
❑ c. P. G. T. Beauregard   ❑ d. Robert E. Lee

8. Future outlaw Jesse James served under which Confederate guerrilla leader during the Civil War?

❑ a. Champ Ferguson
❑ b. William "Bloody Bill" Anderson
❑ c. Merriwether Jeff Thompson
❑ d. Joseph Porter

9. In which state was the 1862 battle of South Mountain fought?

   ☐ a. Virginia   ☐ b. Tennessee

   ☐ c. North Carolina   ☐ d. Maryland

10. What was the full name of General J. E. B. Stuart?

   ☐ a. John Ernst Brown Stuart

   ☐ b. James Ernst Benjamin Stuart

   ☐ c. James Ewell Brown Stuart

   ☐ d. John Ewell Benjamin Stuart

© Stars & Stripes

"Hit th' dirt, Boys!"

11

GENERAL, MULTIPLE CHOICE

1. The fortifications of the Mannerheim Line sat on the border
   between which two countries?

   - ☐ a. Finland and the Soviet Union
   - ☐ b. Denmark and Germany
   - ☐ c. Belgium and Germany
   - ☐ d. Sweden and Finland

2. What caliber is the Thompson submachine gun?

   - ☐ a. .22
   - ☐ b. .33
   - ☐ c. .38
   - ☐ d. .45

3. Which ship mysteriously exploded in Havana harbor in 1898,
   triggering the Spanish–American War?

   - ☐ a. USS *Texas*
   - ☐ b. USS *Indiana*
   - ☐ c. USS *Maine*
   - ☐ d. USS *Massachusetts*

4. Which military commander often rode into battle on his horse,
   Bucephalus?

   - ☐ a. Julius Caesar
   - ☐ b. Alexander the Great
   - ☐ c. William the Conqueror
   - ☐ d. Henry V

5. What kind of firearm was a "harquebus"?

   - ☐ a. matchlock
   - ☐ b. firelock
   - ☐ c. flintlock
   - ☐ d. pinfire

6. What was the operational name for the 1943 Allied invasion of Sicily?

   ❑ a. *Chastise*   ❑ b. *Market Garden*
   ❑ c. *Fortitude*   ❑ d. *Husky*

7. Which American general bore the nickname "Black Jack"?

   ❑ a. Ulysses S. Grant   ❑ b. John J. Pershing
   ❑ c. Dwight D. Eisenhower ❑ d. Douglas MacArthur

8. What type of cannon load contains the greatest number of separate projectiles?

   ❑ a. solid shot   ❑ b. canister
   ❑ c. grapeshot   ❑ d. chain shot

9. "The Desert Rats" was the nickname given to which British armored division?

   ❑ a. 7th   ❑ b. 11th
   ❑ c. 12th   ❑ d. 15th

10. Which country was NOT a member of the Warsaw Pact?

   ❑ a. Romania   ❑ b. Czechoslovakia
   ❑ c. Yugoslavia   ❑ d. Poland

I will not send troops to dangers which I will not myself encounter.
The Duke of Marlborough

GENERAL, SHORT ANSWER

1. The standard Russian BMP-3 was designed to carry how many passengers, in addition to the three crewmembers?

   . . . .

2. What was the greatest number of stars to appear on the battle flag of the Army of Northern Virginia?

   . . . .

3. The War of Jenkins's Ear was fought between Britain and which European rival?

   . . . .

4. The "Flying Fortress" was the name of which American World War II bomber?

   . . . .

5. Which "barbarians" wiped out three Roman legions at the battle of the Teutoburg Forest in AD 9?

   . . . .

6. Officially, how many aircraft did Manfred von Richthofen, "the Red Baron," shoot down in World War I?

   . . . .

7. Which American general plotted the surrender of West Point to the British in 1780?

   . . . .

8. What is the more common name of the "hand-and-a-half" sword?

   . . . .

9. What is the name of the bugle tune played at US military funerals?

. . . .

10. Who was the Roman god of war?

. . . .

© Stars & Stripes

"I need a couple guys what don't owe me no money for a little routine patrol."

QUIZ 6
WORLD WAR I, MULTIPLE CHOICE

1. Which of the following battles was NOT part of the greater "Battle of the Frontiers"?

   ❑ a. Ardennes   ❑ b. Mons
   ❑ c. Lorraine   ❑ d. Somme

2. Which power was not part of the 1882 "Triple Alliance"?

   ❑ a. Germany   ❑ b. Austria–Hungary
   ❑ c. Italy   ❑ d. the Ottoman Empire

3. Which Allied commander captured Jerusalem in 1917?

   ❑ a. T. E. Lawrence
   ❑ b. Charles Dobell
   ❑ c. Edmund Allenby
   ❑ d. Ferdinand Foch

4. The action at Passchendaele was part of which larger battle?

   ❑ a. the Somme   ❑ b. Second Ypres
   ❑ c. Third Ypres   ❑ d. Verdun

5. Who said, "It takes 15,000 casualties to train a major-general"?

   ❑ a. Douglas Haig   ❑ b. Ferdinand Foch
   ❑ c. John J. Pershing ❑ d. Kaiser Wilhelm

6. Which of these tanks had the thickest front armor?

   ❑ a. Mark I   ❑ b. Mark V
   ❑ c. Renault FT-17   ❑ d. A7V

7. Who was King of Belgium during World War I?

    ❑ a. Leopold I   ❑ b. Leopold II
    ❑ c. Leopold III   ❑ d. Albert I

8. After Germany's Manfred von Richthofen, the highest scoring ace of World War I came from which country?

    ❑ a. Germany   ❑ b. France
    ❑ c. Canada   ❑ d. Russia

9. Who was the "savior of Verdun"?

    ❑ a. Philippe Pétain   ❑ b. Ferdinand Foch
    ❑ c. Joseph Joffre   ❑ d. Robert George Nivelle

10. Which nation suffered the most civilian fatalities during World War I?

    ❑ a. Russia   ❑ b. Germany
    ❑ c. France   ❑ d. the Ottoman Empire

DID YOU KNOW?

In 1995, the US Army introduced a new, more environmentally friendly Humvee. Based on elements of the civilian Hummer, the new Humvee featured an engine with greater horsepower but lower emissions, bringing it into line with a 1994 directive from the Environmental Protection Agency.

GENERAL, MULTIPLE CHOICE

1. In 1545, which English warship famously sank within sight of the coast on its way to engage the French?

   ❏ a. *Peter Pomegranate*   ❏ b. *Mary Rose*
   ❏ c. *King Edward*   ❏ d. *Flower of York*

2. What is a "KA-BAR" a type of?

   ❏ a. knife   ❏ b. shovel
   ❏ c. pistol   ❏ d. machine gun mount

3. In which year did the Jews launch their "Great Revolt" against Rome?

   ❏ a. 32 BC   ❏ b. 12 BC
   ❏ c. AD 34   ❏ d. AD 66

4. Who commanded the English fleet that set out to oppose the Spanish Armada in 1588?

   ❏ a. Francis Drake   ❏ b. Lord Effingham
   ❏ d. Richard Hawkins   ❏ d. Martin Frobisher

5. Which warriors most commonly wielded an *assegai*?

   ❏ a. Mongols   ❏ b. Zulus
   ❏ c. Maori   ❏ d. Maasai

6. Napoleon Bonaparte fought in which of the following battles?

   ❏ a. Mount Seleus   ❏ b. Mount Taurus
   ❏ c. Mount Tabor   ❏ d. Mount Tifata

7. By what nickname was Suleiman the Magnificent known to his Muslim followers?

   ❑ a. The Chosen   ❑ b. The Lawmaker
   ❑ c. The Bringer of Fire   ❑ d. The Standard

8. Who was the President of the United States during the War of 1812?

   ❑ a. James Madison   ❑ b. James Monroe
   ❑ c. Thomas Jefferson   ❑ d. John Quincy Adams

9. A "kern" was which type of warrior?

   ❑ a. heavy cavalryman   ❑ b. light cavalryman
   ❑ c. heavy infantryman   ❑ d. light infantryman

10. In which year did the Carthaginians face the Romans at the battle of Cannae?

   ❑ a. 216 BC   ❑ b. 202 BC
   ❑ c. 189 BC   ❑ d. 156 BC

Find the enemy and shoot him down, anything else is nonsense.
Manfred von Richthofen

QUIZ 8

GENERAL, TRUE OR FALSE

1. Edward, "the Black Prince" gained his nickname from the dark armor he wore in battle.
   ❑ True   ❑ False

2. Mustafa Kemal Atatürk fought with distinction at Gallipoli in 1915.
   ❑ True   ❑ False

3. The "Eigranate 39" was a type of German submachine gun used primarily on the Eastern Front.
   ❑ True   ❑ False

4. Wellington was not present at the 1811 battle of Albuera.
   ❑ True   ❑ False

5. The 1690 battle of the Boyne was the last time that King William III and James Stuart (formerly King James II of England) faced each other across a battlefield.
   ❑ True   ❑ False

6. The Principality of Liechtenstein has no standing army.
   ❑ True   ❑ False

7. Benedict Arnold was executed for his attempt to surrender West Point to the British.
   ❑ True   ❑ False

8. Despite repeated efforts during World War II, the Germans were never able to seize the island of Malta.
   ❑ True   ❑ False

9. As part of the 1783 Peace of Paris that ended the American Revolution, Florida became an independent American colony.
   ❑ True   ❑ False

10. Frederick II "the Great" was the grandson of George I of England.
    ❑ True   ❑ False

QUIZ 9

FRENCH AND INDIAN WAR, MULTIPLE CHOICE

1. Who is considered the father of the American Rangers?

   ❑ a. Francis Marion   ❑ b. George Munro
   ❑ c. Robert Rogers   ❑ d. George Washington

2. Which fort did George Washington surrender to the French in 1754?

   ❑ a. Fort Victory   ❑ b. Fort Donaldson
   ❑ c. Fort Washington   ❑ d. Fort Necessity

3. In which year was Louis-Joseph Montcalm killed?

   ❑ a. 1754   ❑ b. 1756
   ❑ c. 1757   ❑ d. 1759

4. During the 1757 siege of Fort William Henry, who occupied the fort?

   ❑ a. American colonials
   ❑ b. American colonials and British regulars
   ❑ c. French Canadians
   ❑ d. French Canadians and French regulars

5. General James Abercrombie was replaced as the British commander-in-chief after his failed attack against which fort?

   ❑ a. Duquesne   ❑ b. Ligonier
   ❑ c. Carillon   ❑ d. Niagara

6. On which side did the Iroquois fight in the French and Indian War?

   ☐ a. French
   ☐ b. British
   ☐ c. Neither, they remained neutral throughout the conflict
   ☐ d. Both, they switched sides halfway through

7. Fort Beauséjour in New Brunswick, Canada, is also known by what name?

   ☐ a. Fort Gaspareaux   ☐ b. Fort Cumberland
   ☐ c. Fort Lawrence   ☐ d. Fort Tintamarre

8. In which year during the French and Indian conflict did France and Britain formally declare war?

   ☐ a. 1754   ☐ b. 1755
   ☐ c. 1756   ☐ d. 1757

9. Who became the head of British military forces in North America upon the death of General Braddock in 1755?

   ☐ a. James Abercrombie   ☐ b. Daniel Webb
   ☐ c. William Shirley   ☐ d. John Campbell

10. What was the first Highland unit to be sent to America during the French and Indian War?

   ☐ a. 42nd Foot, The Black Watch
   ☐ b. Montgomery's Highland Battalion
   ☐ c. Fraser's Highland Battalion
   ☐ d. Cameron Highlanders

GENERAL, MULTIPLE CHOICE

1. Peltasts were ancient warriors primarily armed with what type of weapon?

   ❏ a. bow ❏ b. sling
   ❏ c. javelin ❏ d. axe

2. The Arabic word *askari* is best defined as which of the following?

   ❏ a. sword ❏ b. gun
   ❏ c. soldier ❏ d. horse

3. Which name was given to General Winfield Scott's strategy to defeat the Confederacy?

   ❏ a. the Moccasin Plan
   ❏ b. the Anaconda Plan
   ❏ c. the Boa Constrictor Plan
   ❏ d. the Viper Plan

4. Which militant brotherhood occupied the island of Rhodes for most of the 14th and 15th centuries?

   ❏ a. the Knights Templar
   ❏ b. the Hospitallers of St John of Jerusalem
   ❏ c. the Teutonic Knights
   ❏ d. the Order of Santiago

5. What was the birth name of the Catholic League leader, Graf von Tilly?

   ❏ a. Martin Tserclaes ❏ b. Johann Tserclaes
   ❏ c. Jakob Tserclaes ❏ d. Luther Tserclaes

6. Which World War II German general was known to his soldiers as the "Lion of Defense"?

   ❑ a. Karl Runstedt   ❑ b. Erwin Rommel
   ❑ c. Walther Model   ❑ d. Heinz Guderian

7. What name was given to the American M24 light tank?

   ❑ a. Stuart   ❑ b. Grant
   ❑ c. Chaffee   ❑ d. Sheridan

8. According to the ancient sources, how many war elephants did Hannibal attempt to take across the Alps?

   ❑ a. 18   ❑ b. 37
   ❑ c. 42   ❑ d. 51

9. In which country was it first possible to go "beyond the Pale"?

   ❑ a. Finland   ❑ b. Sweden
   ❑ c. Ireland   ❑ d. Iceland

10. With regards to musketry, what does *feu de billebaud* mean?

   ❑ a. fire at will   ❑ b. volley fire
   ❑ c. rolling fire   ❑ d. fire once and charge

QUIZ 11
GENERAL, SHORT ANSWER

1. Who was the scientific director of the Manhattan Project?

. . . .

2. Which Japanese word roughly translates to "way of the warrior" and generally refers to the code of behaviour of the samurai?

. . . .

3. What does the modern military acronym "IFF" stand for?

. . . .

4. What was the first machine gun fired from an airplane?

. . . .

5. Under the official definition, what is the maximum number of people a "foxhole" was designed to hold?

. . . .

6. What is the famous nickname of Manfred von Richthofen?

. . . .

7. The name of which Native American leader later became the motto of the 501st Parachute Infantry Regiment during World War II?

. . . .

When the last bugle is sounded, I want to stand up with my soldiers.
General John J. Pershing

8. Who won the 1806 battle of Maida, the British or the French?

....

9. Which American general accepted the Japanese surrender in 1945?

....

10. How many American ships were lost at the 1898 battle of Manila Bay?

....

DID YOU KNOW?

When the US Army began to send troops home after World War II, it used a points system to determine priority. Soldiers were awarded one point for every six months of service, plus another point for every six months spent overseas. They received five additional points for each campaign star, each wound, and each decoration. Finally, a soldier was given 12 points for each child he had, up to three. Eighty-five points got a soldier a ticket home.

QUIZ 12

D-DAY, MULTIPLE CHOICE

1. On which beach did the majority of the Canadian forces land on D-Day?

   ❑ a. Gold   ❑ b. Sword
   ❑ c. Juno   ❑ d. Omaha

2. Approximately how many paratroopers were dropped behind enemy lines as part of Operation *Overlord*?

   ❑ a. 5,000   ❑ b. 8,000
   ❑ c. 18,000   ❑ d. 37,000

3. Which two American divisions came ashore in the first wave on Omaha beach?

   ❑ a. 1st and 16th   ❑ b. 1st and 29th
   ❑ c. 16th and 29th   ❑ d. 3rd and 16th

4. Which of the five Allied beaches assaulted on D-Day was furthest east?

   ❑ a. Sword   ❑ b. Juno
   ❑ c. Gold   ❑ d. Omaha

5. The son of which American president received the Medal of Honor for his actions on D-Day?

   ❑ a. Theodore Roosevelt   ❑ b. Franklin Roosevelt
   ❑ c. Herbert Hoover   ❑ d. Calvin Coolidge

France

BILL MAULDIN

"Try to say sumpin' funny, Joe."

6. Which operation occurred first?

☐ a. *Charnwood*   ☐ b. *Goodwood*
☐ c. *Cobra*   ☐ d. *Atlantic*

7. Who was the Deputy Supreme Allied Commander, Allied Expeditionary Forces on D-Day?

☐ a. Betram Home Ramsay   ☐ b. Arthur Tedder
☐ c. Carl Spatz   ☐ d. Bernard Montgomery

8. Who commanded the US 1st Army on D-Day?

   ❑ a. George S. Patton   ❑ b. Dwight D. Eisenhower
   ❑ c. Omar Bradley   ❑ d. Mark Clark

9. Which day of the week was June 6, 1944?

   ❑ a. Monday   ❑ b. Tuesday
   ❑ c. Thursday   ❑ d. Friday

10. The term "D-Day" was first used during which conflict?

   ❑ a. American Civil War   ❑ b. Spanish–American War
   ❑ c. World War I   ❑ d. World War II

Out of the depths of sorrow and sacrifice will be born again the glory of mankind.
Winston S. Churchill

QUIZ 13

GENERAL, MULTIPLE CHOICE

1. Who led the "Green Mountain Boys" during the American Revolution?

   ❑ a. Ethan Allen   ❑ b. Daniel Boone
   ❑ c. Charles Dabney   ❑ d. Edward Anthony

2. Which of Napoleon's marshals was known as "the bravest of the brave"?

   ❑ a. Joachim Murat   ❑ b. Michel Ney
   ❑ c. Louis Davout   ❑ d. Charles Oudinot

3. "Galloglass" were mercenary warriors from which nation?

   ❑ a. Ireland   ❑ b. Scotland
   ❑ c. Spain   ❑ d. France

4. What type of weapon is a "blunderbuss"?

   ❑ a. early rifle   ❑ b. short club
   ❑ c. crude shotgun   ❑ d. multi-barrelled pistol

5. In which year did Julius Caesar cross the Rubicon?

   ❑ a. 51 BC   ❑ b. 49 BC
   ❑ c. 47 BC   ❑ d. 46 BC

6. Which English king was known as the "Hammer of the Scots"?

   ❑ a. Edward I   ❑ b. Edward II
   ❑ c. Edward III   ❑ d. William II

7. In which country was T. E. Lawrence (Lawrence of Arabia) born?

   ❑ a. England   ❑ b. Scotland

   ❑ c. Wales   ❑ d. Ireland

8. In which year was the Special Air Service (SAS) formed?

   ❑ a. 1940   ❑ b. 1941

   ❑ c. 1942   ❑ d. 1943

9. Who was the US Army chief of staff when the Japanese attacked Pearl Harbor in 1941?

   ❑ a. Dwight D. Eisenhower ❑ b. George Marshall

   ❑ c. George S. Patton   ❑ d. Douglas MacArthur

10. Napoleon Bonaparte joined which branch of the French Army?

   ❑ a. infantry   ❑ b. cavalry

   ❑ c. artillery   ❑ d. engineers

"Calm yourself, dear. Even Hitler can't be both dregs AND scum."

GENERAL, TRUE OR FALSE

1. Kamikaze pilots traditionally wore a white headscarf emblazoned with the rising sun.
   ☐ True   ☐ False

2. Iceland became an independent country during World War II, after the German invasion of Denmark.
   ☐ True   ☐ False

3. The Germans were never able to capture Antwerp during World War I.
   ☐ True   ☐ False

4. Over half of all American presidents have served in the armed forces.
   ☐ True   ☐ False

5. As a young man, Prince Frederick (later Frederick the Great) attempted to desert from the military and flee from Prussia.
   ☐ True   ☐ False

6. Ulysses S. Grant fought in the Mexican–American War.
   ☐ True   ☐ False

7. General Andrew Jackson fought the 1814 battle of New Orleans even though he knew that a peace had been signed, officially ending the war with the British.
   ☐ True   ☐ False

8. British general Douglas Haig was made a duke after World War I.
   ☐ True   ☐ False

9. T. E. Lawrence once shot his own camel in the back of the head during a battle.
   ☐ True   ☐ False

10. Genghis Khan is buried in the Genghis Khan Mausoleum.
    ☐ True   ☐ False

ARMIES OF ROME, MULTIPLE CHOICE

1. Where would you find a legionary's *digmata*?

   ❏ a. on his helmet   ❏ b. on his sword
   ❏ c. on his shield   ❏ d. around his neck

2. A Marian legion contained how many cohorts?

   ❏ a. 6   ❏ b. 8
   ❏ c. 10   ❏ d. 12

3. What was the Roman term for a battle line?

   ❏ a. *acies*   ❏ b. *signum*
   ❏ c. *socii*   ❏ d. *orbis*

4. Where did a Roman "Triumph" always end?

   ❏ a. the Temple of Jupiter   ❏ b. the Temple of Mars
   ❏ c. the Temple of Minerva   ❏ d. the Senate

5. Which of the following was NOT one of the Marian reforms?

   ❏ a. uniform weaponry
   ❏ b. mandatory shaving
   ❏ c. inclusion of landless men in the legions
   ❏ d. organization of cohorts

To die by the hand of one's own people is hard.
Field Marshal Erwin Rommel

6. On which part of his body was a legionary most likely to wear a *caliga*?

☐ a. head ☐ b. hand
☐ c. leg ☐ d. foot

7. In a century, who was the "watchword officer"?

☐ a. *centurion* ☐ b. *optio*
☐ c. *cornicen* ☐ d. *tesserarius*

8. According to Polybius of Megalopolis, how were Roman soldiers targeted for decimation killed?

☐ a. beheaded ☐ b. clubbed to death
☐ c. stabbed in the gut ☐ d. hanged

9. Which Roman legion was called the *Ferrata* or "Ironclad" legion?

☐ a. I ☐ b. III
☐ c. VI ☐ d. IX

10. During the republican period, which type of troops formed the smallest maniple in a full-strength cohort?

☐ a. *principes* ☐ b. *triarii*
☐ c. *hastati* ☐ d. *velites*

QUIZ 16
GENERAL, MULTIPLE CHOICE

1. Who was the first commander of the New Model Army?

   ❏ a. Oliver Cromwell ❏ b. Lord Essex
   ❏ c. Thomas Fairfax ❏ d. Philip Skippon

2. In what battle was Confederate cavalry general J. E. B. Stuart mortally wounded?

   ❏ a. Malvern Hill ❏ b. Five Forks
   ❏ c. Yellow Tavern ❏ d. Brandy Station

3. What was the operational name of the British invasion of the Falklands in 1982?

   ❏ a. *Dire Warning* ❏ b. *Corporate*
   ❏ c. *Risky Business* ❏ d. *Terminus*

4. Approximately how many tanks were built in the United States during World War II?

   ❏ a. 20,000 ❏ b. 50,000
   ❏ c. 100,000 ❏ d. 200,000

5. Which country suffered the greatest percentage population loss during World War II?

   ❏ a. the Soviet Union ❏ b. China
   ❏ c. Germany ❏ d. Poland

If there is one thing a dogface loves, it is artillery – his own.
Audie Murphy

---

6. Which of the following best defines a *caisson*?

    ❑ a. small field gun
    ❑ b. wheeled box carrying artillery ammunition
    ❑ c. tool used to clean gun barrels
    ❑ d. type of field fortification for artillery

7. Which country has NEVER been a part of the North Atlantic Treaty Organization?

    ❑ a. Portugal   ❑ b. Finland
    ❑ c. Norway   ❑ d. Hungary

8. Which of the following is NOT a tank-destroyer?

    ❑ a. M3 Stuart   ❑ b. M10 Wolverine
    ❑ c. M18 Hellcat   ❑ d. M36 Jackson

9. Who led the Allied attack on Paris in 1814?

    ❑ a. Lord Wellington
    ❑ b. King Frederick William
    ❑ c. Prince Karl von Schwarzenberg
    ❑ d. Gebhard Leberecht von Blücher

10. St Louis (Louis IX of France) died during which Crusade?

    ❑ a. the Fifth   ❑ b. the Sixth
    ❑ c. the Seventh   ❑ d. the Eighth

QUIZ 17
GENERAL, SHORT ANSWER

EASY

1. What is the lowest rank in the Royal Marines?

   . . . .

2. What is the name for the conflict fought in North America
   during the War of the Spanish Succession?

   . . . .

3. Who wrote *Catch-22*?

   . . . .

4. What is the nickname of the A–10 Thunderbolt II?

   . . . .

5. Is a corvette bigger or smaller than a frigate?

   . . . .

6. Who designed the M1911 pistol?

   . . . .

DID YOU KNOW?

In 1944, Japan attempted to bomb the United States using
large balloons carrying incendiary bombs. The balloons were
released into the jet stream and floated across the ocean.
It is unknown exactly how many balloons reached North
America, though at least 300 are known to have landed in
the United States and Canada. These two countries decided
to keep the balloon offensive a secret, which may have led
to the only casualties – a family from Oregon who
detonated one of the bombs while out hiking.

7. Who won the 1793 battle of Hondschoote, the Allies or the French?

....

8. Which British general famously died defending Queenston Heights from the invading Americans in 1812?

....

9. Which American aircraft carrier was sunk at the 1942 battle of the Coral Sea?

....

10. What is the next line of this famous hymn: "From the halls of Montezuma…"?

....

"…Luger, 100 dollars … Camera, 150 dollars … Iron Cross, 12 dollars …
it is good to be captured by Americans."

SPECIAL FORCES, MULTIPLE CHOICE

EASY

1. Which country's special forces include Task Force 777?

   ❏ a. Jordan ❏ b. Pakistan
   ❏ c. Egypt ❏ d. Kenya

2. In which year did America launch Operation *Eagle Claw*?

   ❏ a. 1979 ❏ b. 1980
   ❏ c. 1981 ❏ d. 1982

3. Which Air France flight was hijacked by members of the PFLP-SOG and landed at Entebbe airport?

   ❏ a. 129 ❏ b. 133
   ❏ c. 139 ❏ d. 147

4. Where is the British Special Boat Service (SBS) based?

   ❏ a. Portsmouth ❏ b. Poole
   ❏ c. Clyde ❏ d. Coulport

5. What nickname is often used for the Greek 1st Paratrooper Brigade?

   ❏ a. the Spearhead ❏ b. the Raider Brigade
   ❏ c. the Night Brigade ❏ d. the Spartans

6. Which actor did NOT appear in the 1990 movie *Navy SEALs*?

   ❏ a. Emilio Estevez ❏ b. Bill Paxton
   ❏ c. Michael Biehn ❏ d. Charlie Sheen

7. Which counterterrorist team was established by the United States Special Operations Group as a precursor to Delta Force?

   ❑ a. Code Black ❑ b. Task Force Orange
   ❑ c. Night Hawk ❑ d. Blue Light

8. In the US military, an "A-Team" or "Operational Detachment Alpha" generally contains how many operatives?

   ❑ a. 4 ❑ b. 6
   ❑ c. 8 ❑ d. 12

9. What is the more colloquial term for the *Sayeret Matkal?*

   ❑ a. the Unit ❑ b. the Team
   ❑ c. the Squad ❑ d. the Base

10. Operation *Acid Gambit* took place in which country?

   ❑ a. Nicaragua ❑ b. Haiti
   ❑ c. Panama ❑ d. Grenada

GENERAL, MULTIPLE CHOICE

1. Which American aircraft carrier was heavily damaged during the battle of Midway, then sunk by a Japanese submarine two days later?

   ❏ a. USS *Hornet*   ❏ b. USS *Yorktown*
   ❏ c. USS *Enterprise*   ❏ d. USS *Saratoga*

2. In which month of 1066 was the battle of Hastings fought?

   ❏ a. July   ❏ b. August
   ❏ c. September   ❏ d. October

3. Who was Tsar of Russia during Napoleon Bonaparte's 1812 invasion?

   ❏ a. Paul I   ❏ b. Alexander I
   ❏ c. Nicholas I   ❏ d. Alexander II

4. Who led the American forces at the 1781 battle of Cowpens?

   ❏ a. George Washington   ❏ b. Daniel Morgan
   ❏ c. Nathaniel Greene   ❏ d. Charles Lee

5. What is the most accurate English translation of *"Al-Qaeda"*?

   ❏ a. the Sword   ❏ b. the Base
   ❏ c. the Warriors ❏ d. the Gun

6. Which of the following nations fielded the most tanks during World War I?

❑ a. Germany   ❑ b. Britain
❑ c. the United States   ❑ d. France

7. Who was the last English monarch killed in battle?

❑ a. Henry V   ❑ b. Richard III
❑ c. Charles II   ❑ d. Henry VI

8. The US Marines earned the nickname "Devil Dogs" during which conflict?

❑ a. the American Revolution
❑ b. American Civil War
❑ c. World War I
❑ d. World War II

9. On September 1, 1939, Nazi Germany invaded which European country?

❑ a. Czechoslovakia   ❑ b. Yugoslavia
❑ c. Denmark   ❑ d. Poland

10. Who was the chairman of the Joint Chiefs of Staff during the First Gulf War in 1991?

❑ a. Colin Powell   ❑ b. David Jeremiah
❑ c. Robert Herres   ❑ d. Norman Schwarzkopf

> *We fight, get beat, Rise, and fight again. The whole Country is one continued scene of blood and slaughter.*
> General Nathaniel Greene

GENERAL, TRUE OR FALSE

1. The outcome of the battle of Chrysopolis in AD 324 brought about the reunification of the Roman Empire under Constantine.

   ❏ True   ❏ False

2. Sir Thomas Picton was wounded in the side by a musket ball during the battle of Quatre Bras.

   ❏ True   ❏ False

© Stars & Stripes

"Nonsense. S-2 reported that machine gun silenced hours ago.
Stop wiggling your fingers at me."

3. Russia and Japan have never signed a peace treaty to end their hostilities of World War II.

   ❑ True   ❑ False

4. Eddie Rickenbacker, America's leading World War I ace, went on to invent the guitar that still carries his name.

   ❑ True   ❑ False

5. Napoleon Bonaparte shot out one of Marshal Ney's eyes in a hunting accident.

   ❑ True   ❑ False

6. German field marshal Walther Model shot himself soon after surrendering to the Allies.

   ❑ True   ❑ False

7. The preferred height for a Roman legionary at the beginning of the Empire was 5ft 6in in modern measurements.

   ❑ True   ❑ False

8. No Polish units fought in the Italian theater in World War II.

   ❑ True   ❑ False

9. The American Civil War featured a battle known in some Confederate sources as "Chickachickaharmony."

   ❑ True   ❑ False

10. Napoleon Bonaparte claimed victory at the 1813 battle of Dresden even though his army was outnumbered by over 70,000 men.

    ❑ True   ❑ False

GENERAL, MULTIPLE CHOICE

EASY

1. After American, what was the most common nationality in the Union Army?

   ☐ a. German   ☐ b. Irish
   ☐ c. English   ☐ d. Canadian

2. Which battle, fought in 1265, saw the end of the Barons' War and the restoration of King Henry III?

   ☐ a. Lewes   ☐ b. Evesham
   ☐ c. Sauchie Burn   ☐ d. Lincoln

3. What type of vehicle was the German World War II "Ferdinand"?

   ☐ a. troop carrier   ☐ b. amphibious tractor
   ☐ c. heavy tank destroyer   ☐ d. self-propelled artillery

4. What nickname was generally applied to Oliver Cromwell's highly trained cavalry?

   ☐ a. Lobsters   ☐ b. Ironsides
   ☐ c. Cavaliers   ☐ d. Dragons

5. Which of these battles took place in a snowstorm?

   ☐ a. Auerstadt   ☐ b. Eylau
   ☐ c. Abensberg   ☐ d. Ladeshut

6. What best describes the shape of a "heater" shield?

   ❏ a. round
   ❏ b. diamond shaped
   ❏ c. straight top with curved sides meeting at a point
   ❏ d. round top with curved sides meeting at a point

7. Which British battlecruiser was sunk by the *Bismarck* on May 24, 1941?

   ❏ a. HMS *Prince of Wales*   ❏ b. HMS *Hood*
   ❏ c. HMS *Suffolk*   ❏ d. HMS *Norfolk*

8. The leader of which nation called "The First Hague Peace Conference" in 1898?

   ❏ a. France   ❏ b. Switzerland
   ❏ c. Germany   ❏ d. Russia

9. Which year saw the first Viking raid on Paris?

   ❏ a. 800   ❏ b. 820
   ❏ c. 845   ❏ d. 880

10. Which of the following is NOT a traditional ingredient of black powder?

   ❏ a. calcium   ❏ b. sulphur
   ❏ c. charcoal   ❏ d. potassium nitrate

QUIZ 22
GENERAL, SHORT ANSWER

1. After which animal was the "culverin" named?

   ....

2. During World War II, did the United States produce more tanks or combat aircraft?

   ....

3. In what battle was Louis-Joseph Montcalm mortally wounded?

   ....

4. What is the meaning of the US Navy acronym "SEAL"?

   ....

5. What does a *mahout* ride?

   ....

6. Which bomber has a bigger bomb capacity, a B-52 Stratofortress or a B-2 Spirit?

   ....

7. What is a "cenotaph"?

   ....

8. Who was born first, Louis II de Bourbon, Prince de Condé or Henri de la Tour d'Auvergne, Vicomte de Turenne?

   ....

9. What was the largest single formation in American military history?

   ....

10. Who had direct command of the above formation?

   ....

QUIZ 23

THE ENGLISH CIVIL WAR,
MULTIPLE CHOICE

1. Which of the following military commanders was NOT present at the 1644 battle of Marston Moor?

   ❑ a. Prince Rupert ❑ b. Prince Maurice
   ❑ c. Sir Thomas Fairfax ❑ d. Oliver Cromwell

2. In which year was the battle of Roundway Down fought?

   ❑ a. 1643 ❑ b. 1644
   ❑ c. 1645 ❑ d. 1646

3. At which battle was General James Chudleigh captured by the Royalists?

   ❑ a. Roundway Down ❑ b. Landsdowne
   ❑ c. Stratton ❑ d. Newbury

4. How old was Sir Thomas Fairfax when he was appointed to command of the New Model Army?

   ❑ a. 33 ❑ b. 37
   ❑ c. 39 ❑ d. 42

5. Oliver Cromwell first had a horse shot out from under him during which engagement?

   ❑ a. Winceby ❑ b. Marston Moor
   ❑ c. Newbury ❑ d. Edgehill

6. Who held command of the Parliamentary horse at the 1642 battle of Edgehill?

☐ a. Sir William Balfour
☐ b. Sir James Ramsey
☐ c. William Russell, Earl of Bedford
☐ d. Oliver Cromwell

7. Which English Civil War battlefield features a place known as "Slash Hollow"?

☐ a. Newbury   ☐ b. Winceby
☐ c. Naseby   ☐ d. Roundway Down

8. Which of the following battles was fought first?

☐ a. Cheriton   ☐ b. Nantwich
☐ c. First Battle of Newbury   ☐ d. Braddock Down

9. After the fall of Bristol to the Royalists in 1643, which military leader was appointed military governor of the city?

☐ a. Prince Maurice   ☐ b. Prince Rupert
☐ c. John Hopton   ☐ d. the Marquess of Hertford

10. In which 1643 battle was Parliamentarian John Hampden mortally wounded?

☐ a. Landsdown Hill   ☐ b. Adwalton
☐ c. Stamford Hill   ☐ d. Chalgrove

GENERAL, MULTIPLE CHOICE

1. In 1941 Moshe Dayan was horribly wounded when he was shot *through* which piece of equipment?

   ☐ a. rifle   ☐ b. canteen
   ☐ c. trumpet   ☐ d. binoculars

2. Which World War II German leader was nicknamed "Sepp"?

   ☐ a. Erwin Rommel   ☐ b. Josef Dietrich
   ☐ c. Heinz Guderian   ☐ d. Wilhelm Keitel

3. Which British army group did Bernard Montgomery command on D-Day?

   ☐ a. 16th   ☐ b. 17th
   ☐ c. 19th   ☐ d. 21st

4. Which commander fought in the most battles?

   ☐ a. Alexander the Great   ☐ b. Julius Caesar
   ☐ c. Hannibal   ☐ d. Napoleon Bonaparte

5. In which year did the "all-big-gun battleship" HMS *Dreadnought* enter service?

   ☐ a. 1898   ☐ b. 1901
   ☐ c. 1906   ☐ d. 1910

Aeroplanes are interesting toys, but have no military value.
Marshal Ferdinand Foch

6. Which member of the Triple Alliance became the first to declare war after the assassination of Archduke Franz Ferdinand?

   ❏ a. Germany   ❏ b. Austria-Hungary
   ❏ c. Italy   ❏ d. the Ottoman Empire

7. Alfred the Great defeated which Viking leader at the 878 battle of Ethandun?

   ❏ a. Halfdan   ❏ b. Harald Bluetooth
   ❏ c. Hartha Hairfoot   ❏ d. Guthrum the Old

8. Which country bombarded Tripoli in 1911?

   ❏ a. the United States ❏ b. Great Britain
   ❏ c. Italy   ❏ d. France

9. What battle was the "Battle of Nations"?

   ❏ a. Baylen   ❏ b. Eggmühl
   ❏ c. Wagram   ❏ d. Leipzig

10. At which battle did the 28th Foot Regiment "The Glosters" win their unique "back badge"?

   ❏ a. Alexandria   ❏ b. Talavera
   ❏ c. Vittoria   ❏ d. Quebec

GENERAL, TRUE OR FALSE.

1. The Red Baron was finally shot out of the sky and killed by ground fire.
   ❑ True   ❑ False

2. Naval "chain shot" did not contain any chain.
   ❑ True   ❑ False

3. The Central Powers had fewer soldiers killed in World War I than the Allies.
   ❑ True   ❑ False

4. The Confederacy had a general whose real name was States Rights Gist.
   ❑ True   ❑ False

5. John Moore, later a lieutenant general in the British Army, did NOT fight in the American Revolution.
   ❑ True   ❑ False

6. Tamerlane was the great-great-grandson of Genghis Khan.
   ❑ True   ❑ False

7. The Romans never used war elephants in their armies.
   ❑ True   ❑ False

8. During the American Civil War, President Abraham Lincoln received several war elephants as a gift from the King of Siam.
   ❑ True   ❑ False

9. It is estimated that over one-third of Wellington's Peninsular Army was made up of Irishmen.
   ❑ True   ❑ False

10. By the end of World War I, American forces were holding a greater percentage of the Allied line on the Western Front than the British.
    ❑ True   ❑ False

SAMURAI, MULTIPLE CHOICE

1. Which of the following terms is nearly synonymous with "samurai"?

   ❑ a. *bushi* ❑ b. *shikken*
   ❑ c. *gekokujo* ❑ d. *kanpaku*

2. What type of weapon is a *yari*?

   ❑ a. bow ❑ b. sword
   ❑ c. dagger ❑ d. spear

3. The Genpei War was fought in which century?

   ❑ a. 12th ❑ b. 13th
   ❑ c. 14th ❑ d. 15th

4. Who was the first samurai to take the permanent title of *shogun*?

   ❑ a. Minamoto Yoritomo ❑ b. Oda Nobunaga
   ❑ c. Yamamoto Kansuke ❑ d. Tokugawa Ieyasu

5. What was the original name of the "Grass-Mowing Sword"?

   ❑ a. Sword of Starry Night ❑ b. Fire-Rain Sword
   ❑ c. Cloud-Cluster Sword ❑ d. Serpent Blade

6. Which samurai created and led "The Red Devils," famous for their red lacquered armor?

   ❑ a. Ishida Mitsunari ❑ b. Kobayakawa Hideaki
   ❑ c. Tokugawa Ieyasu ❑ d. Ii Naomasa

7. What term describes a samurai selected to assist with *seppuku*?

☐ a. *kaishakunin*   ☐ b. *sokotsu-shi*
☐ c. *junshi*   ☐ d. *hara kiri*

8. Who was the eldest son of the *daimyo* Shimazu Takahisa?

☐ a. Iehisa   ☐ b. Toshihisa
☐ c. Yoshihiro   ☐ d. Yoshihisa

9. How many "White Tigers" committed *seppuku* on the mountain Limori-Yama on October 7, 1868?

☐ a. 1   ☐ b. 20
☐ c. 50   ☐ d. 1,000

10. Which of these battles occurred last chronologically?

☐ a. Sekigahara   ☐ b. Mimigawa
☐ c. Nagashino   ☐ d. Kawagoe

DID YOU KNOW?

In 1943, 78 US Marines assaulted the Apamama Islands as part of the Tarawa campaign. Instead of facing a small garrison of determined defenders, they found a number of open graves with the bodies of the Japanese soldiers lying within. It turned out that the leader of the Japanese garrison had accidentally shot and killed himself. The rest of the garrison, following the traditions of the samurai, all took their own lives as well.

GENERAL, MULTIPLE CHOICE

1. Albrecht Wenzel Eusebius van Wallenstein was born within the borders of which modern country?

   ❑ a. Austria   ❑ b. Czech Republic
   ❑ c. Slovakia   ❑ d. Poland

2. In which month of 1917 did the United States declare war on Germany?

   ❑ a. January   ❑ b. March
   ❑ c. April   ❑ d. July

3. Who led the crusaders in their capture of Jerusalem during the First Crusade?

   ❑ a. Robert of Flanders
   ❑ b. Godfrey de Bouillon
   ❑ c. Robert, Duke of Normandy
   ❑ d. Hugh of Vermandois

4. The original "berserkers" were followers of which Scandinavian god?

   ❑ a. Loki   ❑ b. Thor
   ❑ c. Odin   ❑ d. Tyr

5. What term best describes a "petard"?

   ❑ a. polearm   ❑ b. mine
   ❑ c. rope   ❑ d. pistol

6. What was the operational name for the 1980 SAS hostage rescue mission in the Iranian Embassy in London?

- ❏ a. *Lightning*
- ❏ b. *Mercy*
- ❏ c. *Gambit*
- ❏ d. *Nimrod*

7. Which of Napoleon's marshals led the 1807 French invasion of Portugal?

- ❏ a. Jean–Andoche Junot
- ❏ b. Jacques MacDonald
- ❏ c. Nicolas-Jean de Dieu Soult
- ❏ d. André Masséna

8. Which ship was sunk by CSS *H. L. Hunley* on February 17, 1864?

- ❏ a. USS *Albermarle*
- ❏ b. USS *Tennessee*
- ❏ c. USS *Kearsarge*
- ❏ d. USS *Housatonic*

9. What was the typical crew complement for a British Avro Lancaster bomber?

- ❏ a. 6
- ❏ b. 7
- ❏ c. 8
- ❏ d. 9

10. In which American state is Fort Knox located?

- ❏ a. Indiana
- ❏ b. Ohio
- ❏ c. Kentucky
- ❏ d. Illinois

QUIZ 28
GENERAL, SHORT ANSWER

1. AWOL is an acronym for what military phrase?

   . . . .

2. Who wrote *The Influence of Sea Power Upon History*?

   . . . .

3. Which has a higher rate of fire, an AK-47 or an M-16?

   . . . .

4. Which is the higher rank, ensign or midshipman?

   . . . .

5. The CSS *Virginia* destroyed which two enemy warships before its encounter with the USS *Monitor*?

   . . . .

6. In the US Army, what rank comes between major general and general?

   . . . .

7. What was General Ambrose E. Burnside's middle name?

   . . . .

8. In the Middle Ages, which generally had a greater range – the longbow or the crossbow?

   . . . .

9. Who are the "911 Force"?

   . . . .

10. During World War II, did most American tanks run on gasoline or diesel?

   . . . .

QUIZ 29

AMERICAN REVOLUTION, MULTIPLE CHOICE

1. Who famously said, "I have not yet begun to fight!"?

   ❑ a. George Washington ❑ b. "Mad Anthony" Wayne
   ❑ c. John Paul Jones ❑ d. Thomas Paine

2. What was the real name of the infamous "Swamp Fox"?

   ❑ a. Ethan Allen ❑ b. Francis Marion
   ❑ c. Harry Lee ❑ d. Daniel Morgan

3. Which British commander in the American Revolution had "Gentleman" as part of his nickname?

   ❑ a. John Burgoyne ❑ b. William Howe
   ❑ c. Henry Clinton ❑ d. Thomas Gage

4. Where was the "shot heard round the world" fired?

   ❑ a. Lexington and Concord ❑ b. Saratoga
   ❑ c. Bunker Hill ❑ d. Breed's Hill

5. Who was the first commander of the Continental Army?

   ❑ a. Charles Lee ❑ b. George Washington
   ❑ c. Benedict Arnold ❑ d. William Prescott

6. Which of these battles occurred first?

   ❑ a. Princeton ❑ b. Trenton
   ❑ c. White Plains ❑ d. Harlem Heights

. The 1776 battle of Moore's Creek Bridge occurred in which state?

❑ c. Virginia ❑ d. North Carolina

8. General Charles Lee was dismissed from the Continental Army after which battle in 1778?

❑ a. Brandywine ❑ b. Saratoga
❑ c. Monmouth ❑ d. Freeman's Farm

9. What was the name of John Paul Jones' ship when he invaded Scotland and later captured HMS *Drake*?

❑ a. USS *Crusader* ❑ b. USS *Defender*
❑ c. USS *Ranger* ❑ d. USS *Rifle*

10. Brigadier General Johann de Kalb was mortally wounded during which battle in 1780?

❑ a. Camden ❑ b. Cowpens
❑ c. King's Mountain ❑ d. Guilford Courthouse

EASY

ANSWERS

QUIZ 1 GENERAL
1)a 2)c 3)d 4)b 5)c 6)d 7)a 8)b 9)b 10)d

QUIZ 2 GENERAL
1) True. By Cilician pirates in 75 BC
2) False. They met once in 1805
3) True
4) True
5) False. Approximately 50,000 Americans died in Vietnam compared to more than 100,000 in World War I
6) False. It was a dispute in Sicily
7) True. He was 5ft 5in and weighed 112lbs
8) True. The hand belonged to Captain Jean Danjou who died fighting on that day in in 1863 at Camerón, Mexico
9) True
10) False. He was dead last

QUIZ 3 AMERICAN CIVIL WAR
1)d 2)a 3)c 4)b 5)a 6)c 7)c 8)b 9)d 10)c

QUIZ 4 GENERAL
1)a 2)d 3)c 4)b 5)a 6)d 7)b 8)b 9)a 10)c

QUIZ 5 GENERAL
1) 7
2) 13
3) Spain
4) B-17
5) The Germans (Goths)
6) 80
7) Benedict Arnold
8) Bastard Sword (or Longsword)
9) Taps
10) Mars

QUIZ 6 WORLD WAR I
1)d 2)d 3)c 4)c 5)b 6)d 7)d 8)b 9)a 10)d

QUIZ 7 GENERAL
1)b 2)a 3)d 4)b 5)b 6)c 7)b 8)a 9)d 10)a

QUIZ 8 GENERAL
1) True
2) True

3) False. It was a German hand grenade
4) True
5) True
6) True. The closest it has is a national police force
7) False. He died penniless and alone in Britain
8) True
9) False. Florida once again became a Spanish possession
10) True

QUIZ 9 FRENCH AND INDIAN WAR
1)c 2)d 3)d 4)b 5)c 6)b 7)b 8)c 9)c 10)a

QUIZ 10 GENERAL
1)c 2)c 3)b 4)b 5)b 6)c 7)c 8)b 9)c 10)a

QUIZ 11 GENERAL
1) J. Robert Oppenheimer
2) *Bushido*
3) Identification Friend or Foe
4) Lewis gun
5) 2
6) The Red Baron
7) Geronimo
8) The British
9) Douglas MacArthur
10) None

QUIZ 12 D-DAY
1)c 2)c 3)b 4)a 5)a 6)a 7)b 8)c 9)b 10)c

QUIZ 13 GENERAL
1)a 2)b 3)b 4)c 5)b 6)a 7)c 8)b 9)b 10)c

QUIZ 14 GENERAL
1) True
2) True
3) False. Despite staunch resistance by the small Belgian Army, the city fell in October 1914
4) True
5) True
6) True
7) False. Neither side knew that the war was officially over
8) False. He was made an earl
9) True
10) False. His final resting place is unknown

QUIZ 15 ARMIES OF ROME
1)c 2)c 3)a 4)a 5)b 6)d 7)d 8)b 9)c 10)b

QUIZ 16 GENERAL
1)c 2)c 3)b 4)c 5)d 6)b 7)b 8)a 9)c 10)d

QUIZ 17 GENERAL
1) Marine
2) Queen Anne's War
3) Joseph Heller
4) Warthog
5) Smaller
6) John Browning
7) The French
8) Isaac Brock
9) USS *Lexington*
10) To the shores of Tripoli

QUIZ 18 SPECIAL FORCES
1)c 2)b 3)c 4)b 5)b 6)a 7)d 8)d 9)a 10)c

QUIZ 19 GENERAL
1)b 2)d 3)b 4)b 5)b 6)d 7)b 8)c 9)d 10)a

QUIZ 20 GENERAL
1) True
2) True. Although this fact didn't come to light until after his death at Waterloo
3) True
4) False. It was co-invented by his cousin
5) False
6) True. On April 15, 1945
7) False. Preferred legionary height was six Roman feet, or about 5ft 9in–5ft 10in
8) False
9) False. There was a "battle of Chickhominy" in 1864
10) True

QUIZ 21 GENERAL
1)a 2)b 3)c 4)b 5)b 6)c 7)b 8)d 9)c 10)a

QUIZ 22 GENERAL
1) Snake
2) Aircraft, by almost 3:1
3) The Plains of Abraham
4) SEa, Air, and Land

 62

5) An elephant
6) B-52
7) A monument to the fallen, first used in ancient Greece
8) Henri de la Tour d'Auvergne, Vicomte de Turenne
9) 12th Army Group in Europe 1944
10) Omar Nelson Bradley

QUIZ 23 ENGLISH CIVIL WAR
1)b 2)a 3)c 4)a 5)a 6)c 7)b 8)d 9)b 10)d

QUIZ 24 GENERAL
1)d 2)b 3)d 4)d 5)c 6)b 7)d 8)c 9)d 10)a

QUIZ 25 GENERAL
1) True. Australian machine-gunner Sergeant Cederic Popkin probably fired the fatal shot
2) False. It consisted of two iron balls attached by a length of chain
3) True. Over a million fewer
4) True
5) False. He fought with the 82nd Foot
6) False
7) False
8) False. The King did offer the elephants, but Lincoln declined
9) True. The number could be as high as 40 percent
10) True, although only slightly more

QUIZ 26 SAMURAI
1)a 2)d 3)a 4)a 5)c 6)d 7)a 8)d 9)b 10)a

QUIZ 27 GENERAL
1)b 2)c 3)b 4)c 5)b 6)d 7)a 8)d 9)b 10)c

QUIZ 28 GENERAL
1) Absent Without Leave
2) Alfred Thayer Mahan
3) M-16
4) Ensign
5) USS *Cumberland* and USS *Congress*
6) Lieutenant General
7) Everett
8) The crossbow
9) The US Marines
10) Gasoline

QUIZ 29 AMERICAN REVOLUTION
1)c 2)b 3)a 4)a 5)b 6)d 7)d 8)c 9)c 10)a

TWO-STAR GENERAL
KNOWLEDGE

QUIZ 30
GENERAL, MULTIPLE CHOICE

1. Which Scottish king was captured at the battle of Neville's Cross in 1346?

   ❑ a. Robert I   ❑ b. David II
   ❑ c. Robert II   ❑ d. Robert III

2. In which conflict did Mexican general Antonio López de Santa Anna lose his leg?

   ❑ a. Mexican War of Independence
   ❑ b. The War of the Cakes
   ❑ c. The War of Texan Independence
   ❑ d. The Mexican-American War

3. Who led the French at the 1813 battle of Kulm?

   ❑ a. Napoleon Bonaparte   ❑ b. Dominique Vandamme
   ❑ c. Jean-Andoche Junot   ❑ d. Eugene Beauharnais

4. Which US general is sometimes called "The Reluctant Warrior"?

   ❑ a. George Washington   ❑ b. Ulysses S. Grant
   ❑ c. Dwight D. Eisenhower   ❑ d. Colin Powell

5. The "Arrow War" is another name for which conflict?

   ❑ a. Venezuelan War of Independence
   ❑ b. Second Boer War
   ❑ c. Second Opium War
   ❑ d. First Anglo-Afghan War

6. Along with George Armstrong Custer and Wesley Merritt, who was the third of the "Boy Generals" promoted directly from captain to general on June 29, 1863?

❑ a. Elon Farnsworth ❑ b. John Buford
❑ c. Alfred Torbert ❑ d. Philip St George Cooke

7. To whom was Napoleon referring when he said, "That man made me miss my destiny"?

❑ a. Lord Wellington ❑ b. Horatio Nelson
❑ c. William Sidney Smith ❑ d. John Moore

8. Which Gallic tribe did Julius Caesar defeat at the battle of Pontevert (or Axona) in 57 BC?

❑ a. the Suevi ❑ b. the Belgae
❑ c. the Helvetti ❑ d. the Medulli

9. Which of the following was NOT one of "Hobart's Funnies"?

❑ a. Bobbin ❑ b. Centaur
❑ c. Salamander ❑ d. Crab

10. Which of Queen Elizabeth's Sea Dogs "singed the King of Spain's beard" by burning numerous Spanish ships in Cadiz harbor in 1587?

❑ a. John Hawkins ❑ b. Francis Drake
❑ c. Richard Hawkins ❑ d. Martin Frobisher

My only fear is that the Zulu will not fight.
Lieutenant-General Lord Chelmsford

QUIZ 31

GENERAL, TRUE OR FALSE

1. General Frank Merrill, commander of Merrill's Marauders, did NOT attend West Point.
    ❏ True   ❏ False

2. General Norman Schwarzkopf was born with 11 fingers.
    ❏ True   ❏ False

3. The French used parrots perched on the Eiffel Tower to detect incoming aircraft during World War I.
    ❏ True   ❏ False

4. During the American Civil War, the Confederacy had no generals whose last name began with the letter "Z."
    ❏ True   ❏ False

5. The Zulu leader Shaka used to make his soldiers dance in a pit of thorns in order to toughen their feet.
    ❏ True   ❏ False

6. Richard I "the Lionheart" was present at the siege of Acre during the Third Crusade.
    ❏ True   ❏ False

7. The term "gun" derives from "Gunnhildr," a woman's name in Old Norse.
    ❏ True   ❏ False

8. French citizens cannot join the French Foreign Legion.
    ❏ True   ❏ False

9. The Purple Heart medal was instituted by George Washington during the American Revolution.
    ❏ True   ❏ False

10. Originally, the Purple Heart was awarded for "meritorious service."
    ❏ True   ❏ False

AIR WAR, MULTIPLE CHOICE

MODERATE

1. What is the name of the F-106 interceptor?

   ☐ a. Starfighter   ☐ b. Delta Dart
   ☐ c. Delta Dagger   ☐ d. Thunderwarrior

2. What was the only Allied jet aircraft to fly combat missions in World War II?

   ☐ a. F9F Panther   ☐ b. de Havilland Vampire
   ☐ c. P-80 Shooting Star ☐ d. Gloster Meteor

3. Which plane dropped the atomic bomb "Fat Man" on Nagasaki in 1945?

   ☐ a. Enola Gay   ☐ b. Lady Luck
   ☐ c. Bockscar   ☐ d. Silver Lightning

DID YOU KNOW?

Werner Mölders was one of the greatest fighter pilots of all time, and in 1941 he became the first man to top the Red Baron's score of 80 aerial victories. Soon after, he became the first man to score 100. The German High Command, afraid of losing a man who had become a hero to the country, removed him from frontline service and forbade him to fly any further command missions. Condemned to fly as a passenger, Mölders was killed in November 1941 in a plane crash.

DID YOU KNOW?

On March 18, 1945, the aircraft carrier USS *Franklin* was struck by a pair of Japanese bombs, one of which penetrated to the flight deck and set off ammunition and fuel stockpiles. In the ensuing chaos, Chaplain Joseph O'Callahan organized firefighting teams at the same time as administering last rites to hundreds of the dead and dying. For his actions that day, O'Callahan became the first chaplain in US history to win the Medal of Honor.

4. Who was the top scoring Finnish ace of World War II?

   ❏ a. Hans H. Wind ❏ b. Ilmari Juutilainen
   ❏ c. Eino Luukkanen ❏ d. Olva Tuominen

5. During Operation *Allied Force*, a pilot from which nation scored the first aerial victory in the new F-16AM fighter?

   ❏ a. the United States ❏ b. Great Britain
   ❏ c. the Netherlands ❏ d. Greece

6. In 1951 Britain introduced a new maritime patrol aircraft named after which famous explorer?

   ❏ a. Scott ❏ b. Shackleton
   ❏ c. Drake ❏ d. Cook

7. Which nation did NOT have a plane shot down by Major Erich Hartmann?

   ❏ a. the United States ❏ b. the Soviet Union
   ❏ c. Britain ❏ d. France

8. Which aircraft was produced in the greatest numbers during World War II?

- ☐ a. Focke-Wulf Fw 190
- ☐ b. Consolidated B-24 Liberator
- ☐ c. Messerschmitt Bf 109
- ☐ d. Ilyushin IL-2 Shturmovik

9. Which Royal Prussian *Jagdstaffel* was known as "The Red Noses"?

- ☐ a. 18
- ☐ b. 21
- ☐ c. 24
- ☐ d. 27

10. What was the American codename for the Japanese B7A1 bomber?

- ☐ a. Kate
- ☐ b. Jill
- ☐ c. Nate
- ☐ d. Grace

"Here's another complaint about low-flying from the local Archery Club."

GENERAL, MULTIPLE CHOICE

1. In which conflict did the British last wear their traditional red coats in battle?

   ❏ a. Anglo–Zulu War   ❏ b. First Sudan War
   ❏ c. Second Sudan War   ❏ d. World War I

2. Who was the youngest person to hold the rank of brigadier general in the US Army?

   ❏ a. George Armstrong Custer
   ❏ b. Douglas MacArthur
   ❏ c. Galusha Pennypacker
   ❏ d. Colin Powell

3. At the time of the battle of Trafalgar, which of these positions ranked highest in the Royal Navy?

   ❏ a. vice admiral of the blue
   ❏ b. vice admiral of the red
   ❏ d. vice admiral of the white
   ❏ c. rear admiral of the red

4. In which year was Nat Turner's slave rebellion?

   ❏ a. 1823   ❏ b. 1831
   ❏ c. 1846   ❏ d. 1852

He who preaches up a war is a fit chaplain for the devil.
Anonymous

5. Over which river did Horatius make his famous stand on the bridge?

   ❏ a. Tiber   ❏ b. Po

   ❏ c. Arno   ❏ d. Tevere

6. In which battle against Napoleon was Prince Bagration mortally wounded?

   ❏ a. Smolensk   ❏ b. Maloyaroslavets

   ❏ c. Borodino   ❏ d. Mogilev

7. A "misericorde" is what type of weapon?

   ❏ a. dagger   ❏ b. sword

   ❏ c. polearm   ❏ d. crossbow

8. Which US Navy destroyer came under attack in the 1964 Gulf of Tonkin Incident?

   ❏ a. USS *Maddox*   ❏ b. USS *Glavine*

   ❏ c. USS *Smoltz*   ❏ d. USS *Avery*

9. In which battle did Alexander the Great first face the Persian king Darius III?

   ❏ a. Grancius   ❏ b. Halicarnassus

   ❏ c. Issus   ❏ d. Cheronea

10. The special forces unit Force F "Zorros" belongs to which country?

   ❏ a. Nicaragua   ❏ b. Honduras

   ❏ c. Columbia   ❏ d. Mexico

GENERAL, SHORT ANSWER

1. What is the more common name of the battle of Greasy Grass Creek?

   ....

2. The *ocreae* protected which part of a Roman legionary?

   ....

3. King Gustavus Adolphus of Sweden was killed in which 1632 battle?

   ....

4. Which 1877 battle saw "the last stand of the samurai"?

   ....

5. In the US Army, what rank comes between staff sergeant and master sergeant?

   ....

6. Which battle of the American Civil War was fought first, Cedar Creek or Cedar Mountain?

   ....

7. Who designed the AK-47 assault rifle?

   ....

> *The bullet is a mad thing; only the bayonet knows what it is about.*
>
> Field Marshal Prince Aleksandr V. Suvorov

8. How many Nazi leaders were tried at the Major War Crimes Tribunal in Nuremberg?

. . . .

9. Of the above, how many were sentenced to death?

. . . .

10. Of the above, how many were hanged?

. . . .

"Congratulations, Joe—you've completed your fiftieth combat patrol.
We'll put you on mortars for a while."

THE PENINSULAR WAR, MULTIPLE CHOICE

1. Robert Craufurd was buried by the walls of which city?

   ☐ a. Badajoz   ☐ b. Ciudad Rodrigo
   ☐ c. Salamanca   ☐ d. Cadiz

2. Which of the following battles was fought first?

   ☐ a. Nive   ☐ b. Nivelle
   ☐ c. Second Oporto   ☐ d. Orthez

3. Which of Wellington's divisions was known as the "Fighting Division"?

   ☐ a. First   ☐ b. Second
   ☐ c. Third   ☐ d. Fourth

4. Which of Wellington's "exploring officers" was captured in 1812, dined with Marmont, gave his parole, escaped, visited Paris, got an American passport, and returned to Wellington some 18 months later?

   ☐ a. John Walters   ☐ b. Robert Danvers
   ☐ c. Michael Hogan   ☐ d. Colquhoun Grant

5. What caused Sir John Moore's mortal wound at the 1809 battle of Corunna?

   ☐ a. musketry   ☐ b. a saber
   ☐ c. artillery fire   ☐ d. a lance

DID YOU KNOW?

The Congreve rocket system employed by the British throughout much of the Napoleonic wars was so wildly inaccurate that Wellington declared their only use was burning down cities. He did, however, agree to take a unit of rocket artillery in his Peninsular Army, but claimed that he only did so "to get the horses."

MODERATE

6. What was the standard barrel length of the British New Land Pattern "Brown Bess" musket?

 a. 36 inches
 b. 39 inches
 c. 42 inches
 d. 48 inches

7. Which general did Wellington call Spain's "most upright patriot" after his death in 1811?

 a. José de Palafoxy Melzi
 b. Francisco Xavier Castaños
 c. Joaquin Blake
 d. Pedro Caro y Sureda, Marquis of La Romana

8. In which year was the battle of Vimeiro fought?

 a. 1808
 b. 1811
 c. 1812
 d. 1813

9. Of Wellington's seven numbered divisions, which was the only one that did NOT contain a Portuguese brigade?

 a. First
 b. Second
 c. Sixth
 d. Seventh

10. During the Peninsular War, what was the regimental number of the Connaught Rangers?

- ☐ a. 24
- ☐ b. 27
- ☐ c. 87
- ☐ d. 88

"Go tell th' boys to line up, Joe—we got fruit juice fer breakfast."

QUIZ 36
GENERAL, MULTIPLE CHOICE

MODERATE

1. In which battle of the Second Sudan War was General Sir Herbert Stewart mortally wounded?

   ❑ a. Khartoum   ❑ b. Atbara
   ❑ c. El Gubat   ❑ d. Omdurman

2. The navy of which Russian Tsar gained victory over the Swedes at the 1714 battle of Gangut?

   ❑ a. Mikhail   ❑ b. Alexis I
   ❑ c. Feodor III   ❑ d. Peter I "the Great"

3. In which year did a British fleet under Lord Exmouth and a Dutch fleet under Admiral van Capellen bombard the city of Algiers in order to force the Bey to abolish Christian slavery?

   ❑ a. 1810   ❑ b. 1816
   ❑ c. 1824   ❑ d. 1830

4. The American M60 tank is named after which US general?

   ❑ a. George S. Patton   ❑ b. Philip Sheridan
   ❑ c. Ulysses S. Grant   ❑ d. Omar Bradley

I will die in the last ditch.
William of Orange, later William III, king of England

5. Frederick I (Barbarossa) died during which crusade?

   ❑ a. the First   ❑ b. the Second
   ❑ c. the Third   ❑ d. the Fourth

6. Which of the following was NOT used as a defoliant by the Americans during the Vietnam War?

   ❑ a. Agent Orange   ❑ b. Agent White
   ❑ c. Agent Blue   ❑ d. Agent Red

7. What was the earlier operational name of the Allied invasion of southern France, later rechristened Operation *Dragoon*?

   ❑ a. *Hammer*   ❑ b. *Anvil*
   ❑ c. *Scimitar*   ❑ d. *Lance*

8. How many fighting men made up a Mongol *touman*?

   ❑ a. 100   ❑ b. 1,000
   ❑ c. 10,000   ❑ d. 100,000

9. At which battle was General Thomas Graham NOT present?

   ❑ a. Barossa   ❑ b. siege of San Sebastian
   ❑ c. Vittoria   ❑ d. Waterloo

10. What was the theoretical maximum rate of fire of a Gatling gun?

   ❑ a. 200rpm   ❑ b. 400rpm
   ❑ c. 800rpm   ❑ d. 1,200rpm

GENERAL, SHORT ANSWER

1. Who won the 1542 battle of Solway Moss, the English or the Scots?

   . . . .

2. Who was the captain of HMS *Victory* at the battle of Trafalgar?

   . . . .

3. Which US World War II aircraft was nicknamed the "bombing twin"?

   . . . .

4. Which nation lost more ships at the battle of Jutland, Britain or Germany?

   . . . .

5. What is a "snaphaunce"?

   . . . .

6. Who commanded the Ottoman fleet at the 1571 battle of Lepanto?

....

7. At the battle of Actium in 31 BC, whose fleet contained more ships, Mark Antony's or Octavian's?

....

8. How old was General Douglas MacArthur at the time of the Inchon landing in Korea?

....

9. Complete this line by Alfred, Lord Tennyson, "Into the valley of Death rode…"

....

10. About which other Union general did George McClellan write, "He was simply a reckless, gallant boy, undeterred by fatigue, unconscious of fear"?

....

DID YOU KNOW?

In 1908, the Wright brothers went to Washington, DC to try to convince the US military to purchase one of their new airplanes. During the fourth test flight, the plane cracked a propeller and crashed, killing the passenger, Lieutenant Thomas Selfridge, a member of the Army Aeronautical Board that was judging the trials. Less than a year later, the US Army Signal Corps purchased their first Wright brothers' airplane.

QUIZ 38

SPIES, CODEBREAKERS, AND ASSASSINS, MULTIPLE CHOICE

1. Mata Hari was born in which country?

   ❑ a. Denmark   ❑ b. the Netherlands
   ❑ c. Romania   ❑ d. Latvia

2. In 1938 the German spy Herman Lang stole the plans for what secret piece of Allied military equipment?

   ❑ a. American submarine torpedoes
   ❑ b. the Enigma machine
   ❑ c. the Norden bombsight
   ❑ d. British radar

3. Who replaced Thomas Scot as "Director of Intelligence" in 1653 and worked as Oliver Cromwell's spymaster?

   ❑ a. Edward Sexby   ❑ b. Miles Sindercrombe
   ❑ c. John Thurloe   ❑ d. Samuel Morland

4. Dr Benjamin Church, a noted writer of Patriot propaganda during the American Revolution, was actually a spy in the employ of which British military commander?

   ❑ a. General Charles Cornwallis
   ❑ b. General Thomas Gage
   ❑ c. Admiral Richard Howe
   ❑ d. General Robert Howe

5. Which spy, employed by General James Longstreet, first spotted the Union Army advancing towards Gettysburg?

❑ a. Henry Harrison ❑ b. Thomas Jacobs
❑ c. Nathaniel Hawker ❑ d. Nathan Parks

6. In 1939, the British Government Code and Cypher School moved into which Buckinghamshire mansion?

❑ a. Tremington Gardens ❑ b. Tanford Estate
❑ c. Bletchley Park ❑ d. Poppingham Rock

7. In the book of Genesis, Joseph accuses his brothers of being spies from where?

❑ a. Egypt ❑ b. Canaan
❑ c. Rome ❑ b. Babylon

8. Which organization did the famous agent "Stakeknife" spy against?

❑ a. the KGB ❑ b. the CIA
❑ c. the IRA ❑ d. the PLO

9. What was the codename of the World War II German spy Ilyas Bazna, who provided his employers with the codename for the Allied invasion of France?

❑ a. Napoleon ❑ b. Augustus
❑ c. Thor ❑ d. Cicero

10. What was the real name of "Captain Fortescue, gentleman soldier" who plotted to kill Elizabeth I?

❑ a. John Ballard ❑ b. Anthony Babington
❑ c. Gilbert Gifford ❑ d. Bernard Maude

QUIZ 39
GENERAL, MULTIPLE CHOICE

1. Which Latin emperor was captured during the 1205 battle of Adrianople?

   ❑ a. Baldwin I ❑ b. Henry
   ❑ c. Robert I ❑ d. Baldwin II

2. What term was used for a French Resistance fighter in southern France during World War II?

   ❑ a. Maquisard ❑ b. Montagnard
   ❑ c. Hibou ❑ d. Lunard

3. The US Army currently recognizes how many different ranks of warrant officer?

   ❑ a. 4 ❑ b. 5
   ❑ c. 6 ❑ d. 7

4. Which character did Alec Guinness play in the 1957 film *The Bridge on the River Kwai*?

   ❑ a. Commander Shears
   ❑ b. Lieutenant Colonel Nicholson
   ❑ c. Major Warden
   ❑ d. Major Clipton

5. Which Confederate general gave Thomas J. Jackson his nickname when he said "There stands Jackson like a stone wall!"?

   ❑ a. Jubal Early ❑ b. Thomas Green
   ❑ c. Micah Jenkins ❑ d. Barnard Bee

6. Which "Wild West" folk hero also won the US Medal of Honor?

☐ a. Wyatt Earp ☐ b. Wild Bill Hickock
☐ c. Buffalo Bill Cody ☐ d. Jesse James

7. Who did General Douglas Haig replace as head of the British Expeditionary Force in 1915?

☐ a. John French ☐ b. Horatio Kitchener
☐ c. Edmund Allenby ☐ d. Charles Dobell

8. At the 1780 battle of Camden, General Cornwallis defeated which American general?

☐ a. Nathaniel Greene ☐ b. Daniel Morgan
☐ c. Horatio Gates ☐ d. George Washington

9. Which conflict saw the first jet aircraft to be shot down by another jet aircraft?

☐ a. World War II ☐ b. Korean War
☐ c. Vietnam War ☐ d. Six Days War

10. Which conflict saw the battle of Ilipa (also known as Silpia or Elinga)?

☐ a. First Punic War ☐ b. Second Punic War
☐ c. Third Punic War ☐ d. Roman Civil War

Remember this is an invasion, not the creation of a fortified beachhead.
Winston S. Churchill

QUIZ 40
GENERAL, TRUE OR FALSE

1. Winston Churchill escaped from a prisoner of war camp during the Boer War.

   ❑ True   ❑ False

2. In 1401, Tamerlane captured the city of Baghdad and burned it to the ground.

   ❑ True   ❑ False

© Stars & Stripes

3. British general Orde Wingate is buried in Arlington National Cemetery in the United States.
   ❑ True   ❑ False

4. John Paul Jones was the first captain commissioned into the Continental (later the US) Navy.
   ❑ True   ❑ False

5. Charles XII of Sweden was killed in 1708 at the battle of Smolensk.
   ❑ True   ❑ False

6. Before the outbreak of the American Civil War, future Union general Ambrose E. Burnside owned a factory that made breech-loading firearms.
   ❑ True   ❑ False

7. *On War* was not published until after the death of its author, Carl von Clausewitz.
   ❑ True   ❑ False

8. Confederate general Nathan Bedford Forrest never owned any slaves.
   ❑ True   ❑ False

9. Charles de Gaulle escaped from a German prisoner of war camp during World War I.
   ❑ True   ❑ False

10. It is illegal to deploy any military forces to Antarctica.
   ❑ True   ❑ False

QUIZ 41

THE HUNDRED YEARS' WAR, MULTIPLE CHOICE

1. How long was the Hundred Years' War?

   ☐ a. 98 years   ☐ b. 100 years
   ☐ c. 108 years   ☐ d. 116 years

2. At which battle, fought in 1370, were the English under Sir Thomas Granson surprised in their camp and defeated by the French?

   ☐ a. Pontvallain   ☐ b. La Rochelle
   ☐ c. Patay   ☐ d. Formigny

3. How many French "Great Princes" became casualties at the 1346 battle of Crécy?

   ☐ a. 0   ☐ b. 5
   ☐ c. 9   ☐ d. 11

4. Who led the combined forces of England and Burgundy during the 1424 battle of Verneuil?

   ☐ a. Thomas Montague, Earl of Salisbury
   ☐ b. Charles VII
   ☐ c. John, Duke of Bedford
   ☐ d. John Stewart, 2nd Earl of Buchan

5. In which naval battle, fought in 1340, did the English fleet under Edward III and Sir Robert Morley almost completely destroy a French fleet of 70 ships?

❑ a. Brest   ❑ b. Portsmouth
❑ c. Jersey   ❑ d. Sluys

6. How much was the ransom paid by the city of Rouen after Henry V captured it in 1419?

❑ a. 100,000 crowns   ❑ b. 300,000 crowns
❑ c. 500,000 crowns   ❑ d. 1,000,000 crowns

7. Which year saw the signing of the Treaty of Brétigny/Calais in which Edward III gave up his claim to the title of King of France?

❑ a. 1360   ❑ b. 1364
❑ c. 1366   ❑ d. 1372

8. Which battle saw the death of John Joel and the capture of Jean III de Grailli, aka Captal de Buch?

❑ a. Auray   ❑ b. Poitiers
❑ c. Cocherel   ❑ d. Navarrete

9. The 1429 siege of Orléans was led by the English Regent, the Duke of Bedford, and which Earl?

❑ a. the Earl of Cumbria   ❑ b. the Earl of Manchester
❑ c. the Earl of Essex   ❑ d. the Earl of Shrewsbury

10. Which battle, fought in 1367, is also known as the battle of Nájera?

❑ a. Montiel   ❑ b. Auray
❑ c. Navarrete   ❑ d. Patay

GENERAL, MULTIPLE CHOICE

1. In which battle was Edward Bruce, brother of Robert Bruce, killed?

   ❑ a. Bannockburn   ❑ b. Faughart

   ❑ c. Connor   ❑ d. Ardscull

2. What was the first name of Napoleon's father?

   ❑ a. Joseph   ❑ b. Jérome

   ❑ c. Lucien   ❑ d. Carlo

3. The 1862 battle of Oruro was part of which country's civil war?

   ❑ a. the United States   ❑ b. Honduras

   ❑ c. Bolivia   ❑ d. Nicaragua

4. The *Vasilikon Allagia* was the central army of which state?

   ❑ a. the Ottoman Empire   ❑ b. Austria–Hungary

   ❑ c. Byzantium   ❑ d. Prussia

5. What was the average number of crewmen for a regimental cannon in the army of Gustavus Adolphus?

   ❑ a. 2   ❑ b. 3

   ❑ c. 4   ❑ d. 6

6. Which English Civil War commander was given the nickname "The Night Owl" because of his famous night marches?

   ❑ a. Henry Hopton   ❑ b. the Earl of Montrose

   ❑ c. Sir Thomas Fairfax   ❑ d. William Waller

7. Which country was NOT part of the 1718 Quadruple Alliance?

   ❏ a. France   ❏ b. Austria
   ❏ c. Sweden   ❏ d. Britain

8. What type of weapon was a *framea*?

   ❏ a. sword   ❏ b. dagger
   ❏ c. mace   ❏ d. spear

9. Which limb did Fitzroy Somerset, Baron Raglan, lose at the battle of Waterloo?

   ❏ a. his right arm   ❏ b. his left arm
   ❏ c. his right leg   ❏ d. his left leg

10. Which of the following was NOT a southern American partisan leader during the American Revolution?

   ❏ a. Francis Marion   ❏ b. Thomas Sumter
   ❏ c. Ethan Allen   ❏ d. Andrew Pickens

DID YOU KNOW?

Most Viking longships probably carried between 30 and 40 men. However, the Viking kings often wanted something a little more impressive. King Olav Tryggvasson had a ship called "Long Serpent" which could seat 68 men. Not to be outdone, in 1062 King Harold Hardrada launched the "Great Dragon" which featured 35 benches, enough to seat 70 men.

QUIZ 43
GENERAL, SHORT ANSWER

1. Who founded the mountaintop monastery that was destroyed during the 1944 battle for Cassino?

   . . . .

2. Which of Napoleon's marshals was nicknamed the "Duke of Damnation" by the British?

   . . . .

3. RADAR is an acronym for what?

   . . . .

4. Who led the Scots at the 1054 battle of Dunsinane?

   . . . .

5. Which side won the naval battle of Ecnomus in 256 BC, the Romans or the Carthaginians?

   . . . .

6. Who led the Sudanese force that annihilated Baker Pasha's column at the 1884 battle of El Teb?

   . . . .

7. What was the original name of Operation *Yonatan*?

   . . . .

8. What does the "CS" stand for in CS gas?

   . . . .

Anyone who speaks to me of peace without victory will lose his head, no matter who he is.

Adolf Hitler

---

9. Which European battle saw the first recorded use of crossbows since the fall of the Roman Empire?

. . . .

10. In what year was the Second Schleswig War fought?

. . . .

"Aim between th' eyes, Joe—sometimes they charge when they're wounded."

 94

QUIZ 44

THE COLD WAR, MULTIPLE CHOICE

MODERATE

1. In which year did the Soviet Union first detonate a
   nuclear weapon?

   ☐ a. 1946   ☐ b. 1949
   ☐ c. 1952   ☐ d. 1955

2. The Lockheed U-2 spyplane that was shot down over the
   Soviet Union in 1960 carried how many crewmembers?

   ☐ a. 0   ☐ b. 1
   ☐ c. 2   ☐ d. 4

3. Who was secretary-general of the United Nations when the
   resolution to go to the aid of South Korea was passed?

   ☐ a. Trygve Lie   ☐ b. Dag Hammarskjöld
   ☐ c. U Thant   ☐ d. Kurt Waldheim

DID YOU KNOW?

In 1945, Soviet pilot Lieutenant Mikhail Devyataev
and nine of his fellow prisoners managed to escape from
a German prisoner of war camp by stealing a German
bomber and flying it back to Soviet-held territory.
However, the Soviet authorities refused to believe
Mikhail's tale and he spent the rest of the war in prison.
He was eventually made a Hero of the Soviet Union in
1957 after years of "political rehabilitation."

4. The 1962 "Skybolt Crisis" saw a political confrontation between the United States and which of its allies?

☐ a. France
☐ b. West Germany
☐ c. Great Britain
☐ d. Denmark

5. Who was the first air force officer in space?

☐ a. Boris Volynov
☐ b. Andrian Nikolayev
☐ c. Gehrman Titov
☐ d. Yuri Gagarin

6. During the "Corfu Channel Incident," two British destroyers were damaged by mines laid by which country?

☐ a. the Soviet Union
☐ b. Turkey
☐ c. Yugoslavia
☐ d. Albania

7. Which of the following is NOT a type of intercontinental ballistic missile?

☐ a. Medusa
☐ b. Titan
☐ c. Atlas
☐ d. Minuteman

8. Which islands were evacuated by the United States and the Republic of China in 1955 during the First Taiwan Straits Crisis?

☐ a. Yijiangshan Islands
☐ b. Tachen Islands
☐ c. Quemoy Islands
☐ d. Matsu Islands

9. What was the operational name of the Berlin Airlift?

☐ a. *Hot Dog*
☐ b. *Vittles*
☐ c. *Tin Can*
☐ d. *Cook Pot*

10. Who succeeded Nikita Sergeyevich Khruschev as premier of the Soviet Union?

- ❑ a. Nikolai Bulganin
- ❑ b. Leonid Brezhnev
- ❑ c. Georgy Malenkov
- ❑ d. Alexey Kosygin

© Stars & Stripes

"Go ahead, Willie. If ya don't bust it ya'll worry about it all night."

QUIZ 45
GENERAL, MULTIPLE CHOICE

1. What kind of soldiers were *timariots*?

   ❑ a. light cavalry   ❑ b. handgunners
   ❑ c. pikemen   ❑ d. heavy cavalry

2. Who among the following was NOT killed at the 1460 battle of Northampton?

   ❑ a. the Duke of Buckingham
   ❑ b. the Earl of Shrewsbury
   ❑ c. the Earl of Egremont
   ❑ d. the Earl of Warwick

3. Which British cruiser struck a mine on June 5, 1916, killing most of its sailors and passengers – including Horatio Herbert Kitchener?

   ❑ a. HMS *Belfast*   ❑ b. HMS *Sussex*
   ❑ c. HMS *Hampshire*   ❑ d. HMS *Glasgow*

4. How long was the 1648 Turkish siege of Candia?

   ❑ a. 6 years   ❑ b. 13 years
   ❑ c. 18 years   ❑ d. 21 years

5. Who was the last British monarch to lead troops in battle?

   ❑ a. William III   ❑ b. George II
   ❑ c. George III   ❑ d. George IV

6. Which World War II Panzer division was known as "The Bear" Division?

   ❑ a. 1st Panzer Division   ❑ b. 2nd Panzer Division
   ❑ c. 3rd Panzer Division   ❑ d. 4th Panzer Division

7. Where did Winston Churchill NOT say "we shall fight" in his famous speech on June 4, 1940?

   ❑ a. in the hills   ❑ b. in the jungles
   ❑ c. in the streets   ❑ d. on the seas and oceans

8. Which battle of the Wars of the Roses is also called "Loosecoat Field"?

   ❑ a. Bosworth Field   ❑ b. Empingham
   ❑ c. Barnet   ❑ d. Blore Heath

9. What kind of weapon was a Scandinavian *bössar*?

   ❑ a. lance   ❑ b. polearm
   ❑ c. bow   ❑ d. light cannon

10. Which crusader became the first prince of Antioch?

   ❑ a. Bohemund de Hauteville
   ❑ b. Robert of Flanders
   ❑ c. Raymond of Toulouse
   ❑ d. Hugh of Vermandois

They shall not pass.
Marshal Henri Phillipe Pétain

QUIZ 46
GENERAL, TRUE OR FALSE

1. "Scud" ballistic missiles were first fired in combat during the Iran–Iraq War.

   ❑ True   ❑ False

2. The term "Pyrrhic victory" comes from King Pyrrhus' costly defeat of a Roman army at the battle of Asculum in 279 BC.

   ❑ True   ❑ False

3. The Spanish Reconquista ended in the same year that Christopher Columbus made his first trip across the Atlantic Ocean.

   ❑ True   ❑ False

4. *Ronin* is a Japanese term meaning mercenary.

   ❑ True   ❑ False

5. The last German military airship, LZ130 Graf Zeppelin II, was employed for bombing operations in World War II.

   ❑ True   ❑ False

6. Napoleon ordered buttons to be sewn onto the uniform cuffs of his soldiers in order to prevent them from wiping their noses on their sleeves.

   ❑ True   ❑ False

7. Only one British officer present at the battle of Isandlwana survived.

   ❑ True   ❑ False

8. American Revolutionary War general Nathaniel Greene was raised as a pacifist Quaker.

   ❑ True   ❑ False

9. The name of the Mongol warlord "Tamerlane" is actually a corruption of Timur "the Lame."

   ❑ True   ❑ False

10. The firebombing of Tokyo on the night of March 9/10, 1945 caused more civilian deaths than the atomic bomb dropped over Hiroshima.

    ❑ True   ❑ False

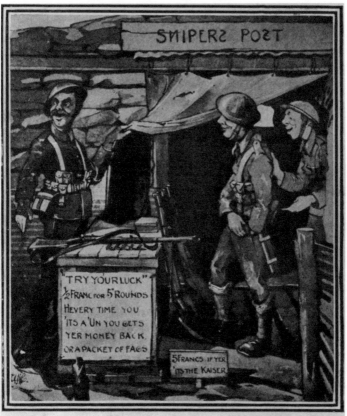

Drawn by 2nd Lieutenant W. H. Clark

QUIZ 47

BIG GUNS, MULTIPLE CHOICE

1. What was the nickname of the "Paris Gun," built by Skoda, and used by the Germans in World War I?

   ❑ a. Emperor William   ❑ b. Big Bertha
   ❑ c. Long Sally   ❑ d. Thor

2. What was the approximate range of "Gustav," the German railroad gun most notable for its use during the siege of Sevastopol in 1942?

   ❑ a. 10 miles   ❑ b. 16 miles
   ❑ c. 22 miles   ❑ d. 29 miles

3. During the 16th century, which of these guns would have normally been the heaviest?

   ❑ a. basilisk   ❑ b. cannon royal
   ❑ c. bastard cannon ❑ d. quarto cannon

4. Which conflict saw the brief use of a "dynamite gun"?

   ❑ a. the Mexican-American War
   ❑ b. the American Civil War
   ❑ c. the Zulu War
   ❑ d. the Spanish-American War

5. What was the primary armament of the King Tiger II?

   ❑ a. 8.8cm KwK 36 L/56   ❑ b. 8.8cm KwK 43 L/71
   ❑ c. 12.8cm PaK 44 L/55 ❑ d. 7.5cm StuK 40 L/48

6. What is the current location of the bombard known as "Mons Meg"?

    ❑ a. London   ❑ b. Edinburgh
    ❑ c. Coventry   ❑ d. Glasgow

7. Which country began construction of the "Babylon Gun" in 1988?

    ❑ a. Iraq   ❑ b. Iran
    ❑ c. Syria   ❑ d. Lebanon

8. The *North Carolina* and *South Dakota* class battleships carried guns of what size as their main armament?

    ❑ a. 9in   ❑ b. 12in
    ❑ c. 16in   ❑ d. 18in

9. What was the largest type of "Parrott rifle" constructed during the American Civil War?

    ❑ a. 50-pounder   ❑ b. 100-pounder
    ❑ c. 200-pounder   ❑ d. 300-pounder

10. Which Russian Tsar commissioned the great "Tsar Cannon" in 1586?

    ❑ a. Ivan IV   ❑ b. Feodor I
    ❑ c. Boris Godunov   ❑ d. Feodor II

Tell the men to fire faster and not to give up the ship. Fight her till she sinks.

Captain James Lawrence

QUIZ 48
GENERAL, MULTIPLE CHOICE

1. By the end of 1813, what was the highest regimental number in use by the French Army?

   ❑ a. 124   ❑ b. 131
   ❑ c. 149   ❑ d. 156

2. In World War II, how many days did the Allied invasion and conquest of Sicily take?

   ❑ a. 9   ❑ b. 19
   ❑ c. 29   ❑ d. 38

3. Which Roman emperor was lynched by legionary recruits in AD 233?

   ❑ a. Maximinus   ❑ b. Severus Alexander
   ❑ c. Aurelian   ❑ d. Elagabalus

4. How old was Gebhard Leberecht von Blücher when he fought the 1813 battle of Lützen?

   ❑ a. 65   ❑ b. 68
   ❑ c. 70   ❑ d. 73

5. Which tribe of Native Americans did Rogers' Rangers attack in the 1759 St Francis Raid?

   ❑ a. Stockbridge   ❑ b. Mohican
   ❑ c. Mohegan   ❑ d. Abenaki

6. What is an "espringald"?

  ❑ a. mobile defensive wall   ❑ b. artillery crossbow
  ❑ c. early type of grenade   ❑ d. type of platemail armor

7. What is the informal name of the SAS's Close Quarter Battle House?

  ❑ a. the Killing House   ❑ b. the Haunted House
  ❑ c. the Slaughter House   ❑ d. the Cider House

8. Operation *Gomorrah* saw the Allies devastate which German city?

  ❑ a. Dresden   ❑ b. Berlin
  ❑ c. Hamburg   ❑ d. Dusseldorf

9. Which general in the Continental Army was also an adopted member of the Native American Mohawk tribe?

  ❑ a. George Washington   ❑ b. Charles Lee
  ❑ c. John Sullivan   ❑ d. Nathaniel Greene

10. In the Byzantine Empire a *theme* was ordinarily commanded by which rank?

  ❑ a. *tribune*   ❑ b. *drungarious*
  ❑ c. *turmarch*   ❑ d. *strategos*

> *It is well that war is so terrible, or we would grow too fond of it.*
> General Robert E. Lee

QUIZ 49

GENERAL, SHORT ANSWER

1. What is the present name of the city of Nicaea, besieged by the Crusaders in 1097?

   ....

2. Which operation included more airborne soldiers, *Overlord* or *Market Garden*?

   ....

3. Who is normally credited as the inventor of "Greek fire"?

   ....

4. Which future US president was wounded during the 1776 battle of Trenton?

   ....

5. What kind of weapon is a "dornick"?

   ....

6. What is the more common name of the 1864 Lopez War?

   ....

7. What was the name of the first nuclear-powered submarine?

   ....

8. Which type of hoplite carried a *sarissas*, *pezetaeri* or *hypaspists*?

   ....

9. Which ship, owned and sailed by Greenpeace, was sunk by the French in 1985?

   ....

10. What is the name of the American F/A-18 multi-role fighter?

    ....

PUNIC WARS, MULTIPLE CHOICE

MODERATE

1. When Cornelius Scipio, later "Africanus," landed in Africa in 204 BC, what did he name his defensive camp?

   ❑ a. Castra Lucretia   ❑ b. Castra Donella
   ❑ c. Castra Ophelia   ❑ d. Castra Cornelia

2. The Third Punic War began in 149 BC, but when did it end?

   ❑ a. 147 BC   ❑ b. 146 BC
   ❑ c. 145 BC   ❑ d. 143 BC

3. How did Hamilcar Barca die?

   ❑ a. he was beheaded   ❑ b. he was poisoned
   ❑ c. he drowned   ❑ d. he was shot by an arrow

4. From which city did Hannibal set off on his march across the Alps in 218 BC?

   ❑ a. Carthage   ❑ b. New Carthage
   ❑ c. Dertosa   ❑ d. Baecula

5. During the Punic Wars, a full-strength Roman legion contained how many cavalry troopers?

   ❑ a. 0   ❑ b. 100
   ❑ c. 300   ❑ d. 600

6. Which Roman consul held command of the Roman army that faced Hannibal on the day before the 216 BC battle of Cannae?

   ❑ a. Terentius Varro   ❑ b. Gaius Flaminius
   ❑ c. Gnaeus Servilius   ❑ d. Aemilius Paullus

7. The Second Punic War ended with Carthage agreeing to pay Rome 10,000 talents over a period of how many years?

   ❑ a. 5   ❑ b. 10
   ❑ c. 50   ❑ d. 100

8. The Punic Wars began with the breaking of which "Treaty of Friendship"?

   ❑ a. First   ❑ b. Second
   ❑ c. Third   ❑ d. Fourth

9. How many elephants did Hannibal have at the battle of Zama in 202 BC?

   ❑ a. 0   ❑ b. 30
   ❑ c. 80   ❑ d. 110

10. In which year was Hannibal born?

   ❑ a. 259 BC   ❑ b. 255 BC
   ❑ c. 252 BC   ❑ d. 247 BC

Peace is going to be hell on me.
General George S. Patton

QUIZ 51
GENERAL, MULTIPLE CHOICE

MODERATE

1. Who won the 1643 battle of Rocroi?

   ❑ a. Spain   ❑ b. France
   ❑ c. Italy   ❑ d. Denmark

2. The famous mercenary Pipo Spano (or Pipo of Ozora) was born in which country?

   ❑ a. Italy   ❑ b. Hungary
   ❑ c. Serbia   ❑ d. Bulgaria

3. Where did John Churchill, Duke of Marlborough and Prince Eugene of Savoy meet for the first time?

   ❑ a. Blenheim   ❑ b. Oudernarde
   ❑ c. Malplaquet   ❑ d. Mundelsheim

4. Which conflict saw the US launch Operation *Ripper*?

   ❑ a. Korean War   ❑ b. Cuban Missile Crisis
   ❑ c. Vietnam War   ❑ d. the Bay of Pigs

5. Erich von Manstein was what relation to Paul von Hindenburg?

   ❑ a. none   ❑ b. his cousin
   ❑ c. his brother-in-law ❑ d. his nephew

6. How many submarines participated in the 1916 battle of Jutland?

   ❑ a. 0   ❑ b. 1
   ❑ c. 8   ❑ d. 23

7. A *sulitsi* is what type of weapon?

   ❑ a. rifle   ❑ b. sword
   ❑ c. javelin   ❑ d. throwing axe

8. In which country did the Allies launch Operation *Crawdad* in World War II?

   ❑ a. France   ❑ b. Egypt
   ❑ c. Italy   ❑ d. Germany

9. The term *Gourmier* refers to a soldier from which nation?

   ❑ a. Tunisia   ❑ b. Algeria
   ❑ c. Morocco   ❑ d. Libya

10. Who was the first Commander-in-Chief of the Fleet of the Continental Navy?

   ❑ a. John Barry   ❑ b. Esek Hopkins
   ❑ c. Nicholas Biddle ❑ d. Joshua Barney

DID YOU KNOW?

The German commander Paul von Lettow-Vorbeck ran rings around British forces in Africa during World War I, and returned to Germany in 1919 as an undefeated hero. Distrustful of Hitler, Lettow-Vorbeck managed to remain on the sidelines during World War II even though both of his sons died in the fighting. During the economic collapse in Germany after the war, Lettow-Vorbeck managed to survive by carving wooden statues and receiving regular food parcels from his former British enemies in Africa.

QUIZ 52

GENERAL, TRUE OR FALSE

1. Subatai Ba'adur died just weeks before his leader, Genghis Khan.
   ☐ True   ☐ False

2. Over 20 Allied soldiers were killed during the invasion of the Aleutian island of Kiska, despite the fact that there was no enemy present.
   ☐ True   ☐ False

MODERATE

"Sure I got seniority. I got busted a week before you did."

111

3. Emperor Claudius defeated the invading Goths at the battle of Naissus in AD 269.

❑ True   ❑ False

4. After fighting for the Americans during the Revolution, the Marquis de Lafayette ended up spending nearly five years as a captive of the Austrians and Prussians.

❑ True   ❑ False

5. George S. Patton won the Nobel Peace Prize.

❑ True   ❑ False

6. Sir John Moore was once saved from death when a musket ball deflected off the telescope he was holding.

❑ True   ❑ False

7. The US government had a plan to blame Castro if the 1962 Mercury space mission crashed.

❑ True   ❑ False

8. Fewer than 100 soldiers died on the final day of World War I.

❑ True   ❑ False

9. The first plane to make a non-stop around-the-world flight was a Russian bomber.

❑ True   ❑ False

10. The M26 Pershing tank arrived too late to see action in the Pacific theater.

❑ True   ❑ False

...no firing until you see the whites of their eyes.
Frederick the Great

QUIZ 53

WAR IN THE PACIFIC, MULTIPLE CHOICE

1. How many ships were sunk during the 1944 battle of Leyte Gulf?

   ❏ a. 2   ❏ b. 10
   ❏ c. 22   ❏ d. 32

2. Which Pacific island saw the largest *banzai* charge of the war?

   ❏ a. Iwo Jima   ❏ b. Tarawa
   ❏ c. Leyte   ❏ d. Saipan

3. Which American aircraft carrier launched James H. Doolittle and his B-25 bombers on their famous raid on mainland Japan?

   ❏ a. USS *Enterprise*   ❏ b. USS *Hornet*
   ❏ c. USS *Yorktown*   ❏ d. USS *Lexington*

4. How many submarines did the Japanese lose during the attack on Pearl Harbor?

   ❏ a. 0   ❏ b. 2
   ❏ c. 4   ❏ d. 6

5. What was the official Allied name for the Japanese night resupply missions that the American press dubbed the "Tokyo Express"?

   ❏ a. Pineapple Express   ❏ b. Banana Express
   ❏ c. Cactus Express   ❏ d. Peanut Express

6. How many B–25B Mitchell bombers participated in the Doolittle Raid?

  ❏ a. 10   ❏ b. 12
  ❏ c. 16   ❏ d. 20

7. What was the daily ration of cigarettes for American soldiers in the Pacific theater?

  ❏ a. 0   ❏ b. 10
  ❏ c. 20   ❏ d. 50

8. Which Imperial Japanese admiral became Commander-in-Chief of the Combined Fleet after the death of Isoroku Yamamoto in 1943?

  ❏ a. Mineichi Koga   ❏ b. Takeo Kurita
  ❏ c. Sentaro Omori   ❏ d. Nobutake Kondo

9. Which of these battles occurred last, chronologically?

  ❏ a. the battle of Kolombangara
  ❏ b. the battle of Vela Gulf
  ❏ c. the battle of Empress Augusta Bay
  ❏ d. the battle of Cape St George

10. Which of these Japanese aircraft carriers was NOT present at the battle of the Coral Sea?

  ❏ a. *Shoto*   ❏ b. *Akagi*
  ❏ c. *Shokaku*   ❏ d. *Zuikaku*

GENERAL, MULTIPLE CHOICE

1. In what year was the Minié bullet invented?

   ❑ a. 1832   ❑ b. 1837
   ❑ c. 1840   ❑ d. 1849

2. According to the Duke of Wellington (or Blücher, depending on your source) Napoleon's presence on the battlefield was worth how many men?

   ❑ a. 10,000   ❑ b. 20,000
   ❑ c. 30,000   ❑ d. 40,000

3. The 1943 "Palm Sunday Goose Shoot" occurred in the skies over which country?

   ❑ a. Libya   ❑ b. Tunisia
   ❑ c. Egypt   ❑ d. Italy

4. Which country was not a founding member of the 1912 Balkan League?

   ❑ a. Albania   ❑ b. Bulgaria
   ❑ c. Serbia   ❑ d. Greece

5. Which of the following best describes a "roundelad"?

   ❑ a. a hooked polearm
   ❑ b. a shield with a rounded bottom but square top
   ❑ c. a primitive type of cannon
   ❑ d. a military ship designed for ramming and boarding

6. Which of these battles in the Sioux and Northern Cheyenne War of 1876–77 occurred first?

   ❑ a. Rosebud   ❑ b. Powder River
   ❑ c. Little Big Horn   ❑ d. Wolf Mountains

7. Approximately how many men formed the English contingent led by John Churchill, Duke of Marlborough, at the 1698 battle of Walcourt?

   ❑ a. 2,000   ❑ b. 4,000
   ❑ c. 8,000   ❑ d. 12,000

8. What year saw the opening of the "Washington Conference" in which the leading naval powers agreed to numerous arms limitation measures?

   ❑ a. 1921   ❑ b. 1924
   ❑ c. 1927   ❑ d. 1931

9. Which Charles was defeated by the Vikings at the 852 battle of Givald's Foss?

   ❑ a. Charles the Simple   ❑ b. Charles the Fat
   ❑ c. Charles the Bald   ❑ d. Charles the Great

10. Which English monarch knighted Henry Morgan after his raids on Panama?

   ❑ a. Charles II   ❑ b. James II
   ❑ c. William III ❑ d. Queen Anne

Brave men die in battle.
Major-General William S. Rosencrans

GENERAL, TRUE OR FALSE

1. On D-Day, General Patton was busy inspecting a non-existent army.
   ❏ True   ❏ False

2. During the battle of Borodino, over 50 generals in Napoleon's army became casualties.
   ❏ True   ❏ False

"Beautiful view. Is there one for the enlisted men?"

3. The Great White Fleet circumnavigated the globe between 1907 and 1909.
   ❏ True   ❏ False

4. The body of John Paul Jones was lost for nearly 100 years before being rediscovered in an animal graveyard.
   ❏ True   ❏ False

5. Hernando Cortez scuttled his own fleet in Mexico to prevent desertions.
   ❏ True   ❏ False

6. Over half the bombs dropped by the Argentinians during the Falklands War failed to explode.
   ❏ True   ❏ False

7. No actual combat occurred between the Americans and Japanese on the Aleutian Islands during World War II.
   ❏ True   ❏ False

8. No British or Commonwealth soldiers were executed for mutiny during World War II.
   ❏ True   ❏ False

9. Nearly 100,000 soldiers fought in the 1854 battle of Alma, and over 20,000 were wounded.
   ❏ True   ❏ False

10. More Americans became battle casualties on September 17, 1862, than on any other day.
    ❏ True   ❏ False

My wounded are behind me and I will never pass them alive.
Major-General Zachary Taylor, on receiving the order to retreat during the battle of Buena Vista, 1847

QUIZ 56
VICTORIA'S WARS, MULTIPLE CHOICE

1. Who led the charge of the Light Brigade?

   ☐ a. Colin Campbell   ☐ b. James Thomas Brudenell
   ☐ c. William Howard Russell ☐ d. James Simpson

2. In which battle was General William Hicks' column of 10,000
   Egyptians completely wiped out by the forces of the Mahdi?

   ☐ a. Tel el-Kebir   ☐ b. El Obeid
   ☐ c. El Teb   ☐ d. Abu Hamed

3. Which month in 1885 saw the fall of Khartoum and the death
   of General Gordon?

   ☐ a. January   ☐ b. February
   ☐ c. March   ☐ d. April

DID YOU KNOW?

In January 1942, Adolf Galland was awarded Germany's
highest gallantry award, the Knight's Cross with Diamonds, in
recognition for his 92 aerial victories. Soon afterward, Herman
Göring saw the award, decided the diamonds looked fake, and
replaced it with a higher-quality version. When Hitler heard
about the incident, he too provided a replacement. Thus
Galland became probably the only man in history to be
presented with two sets of this extremely rare medal.

4. Which year saw the outbreak of the Second Maori War?

- ☐ a. 1850
- ☐ b. 1855
- ☐ c. 1860
- ☐ d. 1865

5. What was the name of the missionary who ran the mission at Rorke's Drift at the time of the battle?

- ☐ a. Ferdnand Schiess
- ☐ b. Christian Kugler
- ☐ c. Otto Witt
- ☐ d. Samuel Gobat

6. Who led the British relief column to Kandahar in 1880?

- ☐ a. Louis Cavagnari
- ☐ b. Frederick Roberts
- ☐ c. G. R. S. Burroughs
- ☐ d. James Primrose

7. What was the birth name of Sir Henry Morton Stanley?

- ☐ a. John Rowlands
- ☐ b. Henry Hopton
- ☐ c. David Griffith
- ☐ d. David Jones

8. Between 1852 and 1900, how many wars did Britain fight in Burma?

- ☐ a. 0
- ☐ b. 1
- ☐ c. 2
- ☐ d. 3

9. The short "Gun War" erupted in South Africa in which year?

- ☐ a. 1865
- ☐ b. 1872
- ☐ c. 1880
- ☐ d. 1889

10. In which country was the 1868 battle of Arogee fought?

- ☐ a. Egypt
- ☐ b. Sudan
- ☐ c. Ethiopia
- ☐ d. South Africa

QUIZ 57
GENERAL, MULTIPLE CHOICE

1. Which Japanese aircraft carrier was NOT present at the 1942 battle of Midway?

   ❑ a. *Akagi*   ❑ b. *Hiryu*
   ❑ c. *Soryu*   ❑ d. *Shokaku*

2. Which ship was Horatio Nelson's first command?

   ❑ a. HMS *Lowestoft*   ❑ b. HMS *Badger*
   ❑ c. HMS *Triumph*   ❑ d. HMS *Seahorse*

3. How many assassination attempts is Hitler known to have survived between 1933 and 1945?

   ❑ a. 6   ❑ b. 7
   ❑ c. 8   ❑ d. 10

4. Which army did not use the rank of *taxiarch*?

   ❑ a. Macedonian   ❑ b. Spartan
   ❑ c. Athenian   ❑ d. Byzantine

5. The beginning of the German "Second Reich" is usually dated from the ascension of which ruler?

   ❑ a. Wilhelm I   ❑ b. Frederick III
   ❑ c. Wilhelm II   ❑ d. Friedrich Ebert

There are no manifestos like cannon and musketry.
The Duke of Wellington

6. Which conflict saw the United States launch Operation *Peace Arrow*?

☐ a. Vietnam War ☐ b. Korean War
☐ c. the invasion of Panama ☐ d. the invasion of Grenada

7. Which part of the body is protected by a *cabacete*?

☐ a. arms ☐ b. legs
☐ c. chest ☐ d. head

8. Which ruler was sometimes known as "The Sergeant King"?

☐ a. Frederick William II of Prussia
☐ b. Frederick I of Prussia
☐ c. Frederick William I of Prussia
☐ d. Frederick II of Prussia

9. In which year was the British Territorial Force created?

☐ a. 1898 ☐ b. 1904
☐ c. 1908 ☐ d. 1914

10. Which weapon was nicknamed "The right arm of the Free World"?

☐ a. M-16 assault rifle ☐ b. FN FAL battle rifle
☐ c. M60 machine gun ☐ d. M1918 BAR automatic rifle

Between a battle lost and a battle won, the distance is immense and there stand empires.
Napoleon Bonaparte

GENERAL, SHORT ANSWER

1. Who was Abraham Lincoln's first vice-president?

   ....

2. Which Hussite leader was known for only having one eye?

   ....

3. Which battle during the American Revolution featured only one British soldier?

   ....

4. Who wrote the *Treatise on Great Military Operations* and *Summary of the Art of War*?

   ....

5. Which country invaded Honduras in 1907?

   ....

6. What is the name of the only dynamite gun cruiser in the history of the US Navy?

   ....

7. What is the oldest chartered military organization in the United States that is still active?

   ....

8. In what year did Austria regain its independence after World War II?

   ....

9. Which ancient general was the first commander known to have used field artillery?

   ....

10. Of the brothers, Hengist and Horsa, which was slain at the 455 BC battle of Aegelsthrep?

    ....

MODERATE

GENERAL, MULTIPLE CHOICE

1. Who first officially used the term "Axis" to define the alliance between Germany and Italy in the days leading up to World War II?

   ❑ a. Adolf Hitler ❑ b. Benito Mussolini
   ❑ c. Ion Antonescu ❑ d. Bogdan Filov

2. Which ship served as Admiral Dewey's flagship during the 1898 battle of Manila Bay?

   ❑ a. USS *Baltimore* ❑ b. USS *Olympia*
   ❑ c. USS *Raleigh* ❑ d. USS *Boston*

3. In which year did the Japanese sink the USS *Panay* in an unprovoked attack as the boat was moored near Nanking?

   ❑ a. 1933 ❑ b. 1935
   ❑ c. 1937 ❑ d. 1939

4. Which conflict did Winston Churchill describe as the first "world war"?

   ❑ a. War of the Spanish Succession
   ❑ b. War of the Austrian Succession
   ❑ c. Seven Years' War
   ❑ d. Queen Anne's War

5. Which operation did Israel launch as a reaction to the 1972 Munich massacre?

   ❑ a. *Justice of Solomon* ❑ b. *Thunder Strike*
   ❑ c. *Sword of Gideon* ❑ d. *Wrath of God*

6. Which Australian aircraft carrier cut the US destroyer *Franklin E. Evans* in half during a 1969 exercise?

❑ a. HMAS *Kanimbla*
❑ b. HMAS *Melbourne*
❑ c. HMAS *Vengence*
❑ d. HMAS *Sydney*

7. Private military consultant, Tim Spicer, was formerly an officer of which British regiment?

❑ a. Grenadier Guards
❑ b. Royal Green Jackets
❑ c. Worcestershire and Sherwood Foresters
❑ d. Scots Guards

8. Operation *Z* is another name for which attack?

❑ a. Pearl Harbor, 1941
❑ b. the Doolittle Raid, 1942
❑ b. the atomic bombing of Hiroshima, 1945
❑ d. the atomic bombing of Nagasaki, 1945

9. What was the operational name for the 1956 Anglo-French invasion of Suez?

❑ a. *Musketeer*   ❑ b. *Lancer*
❑ c. *Razor*   ❑ d. *Scythe*

10. In which city was James Graham, 1st Marquis of Montrose, executed?

❑ a. London   ❑ b. Paris
❑ c. Edinburgh   ❑ d. York

GENERAL, SHORT ANSWER

1. Who won the 1904 naval battle of Che-mul-pho, the Russians or the Japanese?

   . . . .

2. According to Union commander General Sherman, which Confederate general "must be hunted down if it costs ten thousand lives and bankrupts the Federal treasury"?

   . . . .

3. Who became Chief of the High Command of the Armed Forces in Germany in 1939?

   . . . .

4. Who was taller, George Washington or Andrew Jackson?

   . . . .

5. Who led the Viet Minh during the 1954 battle of Dien Bien Phu?

   . . . .

6. Which famous author, working as a field reporter, covered the American charge up San Juan Hill in 1898?

   . . . .

7. *Niitakayama Nobore* or "climb Mount Niitaka" was the signal for what?

   . . . .

8. Which Spanish military leader is known as "The Great Captain"?

....

9. Which battle of the Hundred Years' War was ostensibly fought over salted fish?

....

10. Heinz Guderian described himself as the pupil and disciple of which British military theorist?

....

US PRESIDENTS, MULTIPLE CHOICE

1. Who is the only US president to have served in the regular army and never obtained a rank higher than private?

   ☐ a. Millard Philmore   ☐ b. John Tyler
   ☐ c. James Buchanan   ☐ d. Calvin Coolidge

2. Which of the following enemies did Zachary Taylor never meet on the battlefield?

   ☐ a. British regulars   ☐ b. Black Hawk warriors
   ☐ c. Seminole warriors   ☐ d. Mexican regulars

3. How many Civil War generals later became President of the United States?

   ☐ a. 2   ☐ b. 4
   ☐ c. 5   ☐ d. 6

4. Who was the first US president to have served in the navy?

   ☐ a. Rutherford B. Hayes   ☐ b. Harry S. Truman
   ☐ c. John F. Kennedy   ☐ d. Richard Nixon

DID YOU KNOW?

The Tsar Cannon is one of the largest bombards ever constructed. Commissioned in 1586 by Tsar Feodor and constructed by Andrey Chokhov, it was designed to fire stone grapeshot weighing over 500kg. The cannon was placed as part of the defense of Moscow, but has never been fired.

5. Which future president crossed the Delaware with George Washington on December 25, 1776?

❑ a. John Adams ❑ b. James Madison
❑ c. John Quincy Adams ❑ d. James Monroe

6. Ulysses S. Grant was which President of the United States?

❑ a. 14th ❑ b. 16th
❑ c. 18th ❑ d. 21st

7. Which president served as Quartermaster General of the US Army?

❑ a. Rutherford B. Hayes ❑ b. Chester A. Arthur
❑ c. Grover Cleveland ❑ d. James A. Garfield

8. Which president was sometimes known as "Old Rough and Ready"?

❑ a. Theodore Roosevelt ❑ b. Andrew Jackson
❑ c. George Washington ❑ d. Zachary Taylor

9. Which president authorized the American special forces to officially – and exclusively – wear the green beret?

❑ a. Dwight D. Eisenhower ❑ b. Richard Nixon
❑ c. John F. Kennedy ❑ d. Lyndon B. Johnson

10. What rank did Ronald Reagan reach in the US Army?

❑ a. lieutenant ❑ b. captain
❑ c. major ❑ d. he was never in the army

GENERAL, MULTIPLE CHOICE

1. During which battle was Winfield Scott captured by the British?

   ❑ a. Queenston Heights ❑ b. Burlington Heights
   ❑ c. Chippewa ❑ d. Chrysler's Farm

2. What was Julius Caesar's last battle?

   ❑ a. Mutina ❑ b. Munda
   ❑ c. Zela ❑ d. Treveri

3. Johann Tserclaes, Graf von Tilly was mortally wounded during the defense of which river?

   ❑ a. Rhine ❑ b. Oder
   ❑ c. Weser ❑ d. Lech

4. Which Greek general led his forces to disaster at the battle of Coronea in 447 BC?

   ❑ a. Pausanias ❑ b. Mardonius
   ❑ c. Tolmides ❑ d. Aminias

5. Which 1782 naval battle is also known as "the battle of the Saints"?

   ❑ a. Grenada ❑ b. Porto Praia Bay
   ❑ c. Dogger Bank ❑ d. Dominica

Retreat, hell! We just got over here.
Major-General Wendell Neville

6. The government of which nation awarded the Wright brothers their first medals?

   ❑ a. the United States   ❑ b. Great Britain
   ❑ c. France   ❑ d. Germany

7. According to Winston Churchill, which battle was England's greatest victory over France?

   ❑ a. Waterloo   ❑ b. Agincourt
   ❑ c. Poitiers   ❑ d. Crécy

8. A Dacian *falce* or *falx* is most similar to which other type of weapon?

   ❑ a. morning star   ❑ b. warhammer
   ❑ c. scythe   ❑ d. compound bow

9. In which year did the First Mysore War begin?

   ❑ a. 1756   ❑ b. 1766
   ❑ c. 1772   ❑ d. 1778

10. Which military officer led the successful 1953 Everest expedition?

   ❑ a. John Hunt   ❑ b. Edmund Hillary
   ❑ c. George Lowe   ❑ d. Charles Evans

GENERAL, TRUE OR FALSE

1. At the end of World War I, most of the German High Seas Fleet sailed to Portsmouth as part of the armistice.
   ❏ True   ❏ False

2. Finland has never had a civil war.
   ❏ True   ❏ False

3. The German general Paul von Lettow-Vorbeck, hero of Africa in World War I, died during World War II.
   ❏ True   ❏ False

4. The island of Martinique was seized from the French in both the French Revolutionary Wars and the Napoleonic Wars, only to be restored to France in 1814.
   ❏ True   ❏ False

5. As a young soldier, Winfield Scott was court-martialled and suspended from the army.
   ❏ True   ❏ False

6. Queen Isabella I of Castile often accompanied her army in the field, clad in armor.
   ❏ True   ❏ False

7. Geronimo was an Apache chieftain.
   ❏ True   ❏ False

DID YOU KNOW?

During the siege of Jaffa in 1799, a musket ball knocked the hat off Napoleon Bonaparte and killed the taller colonel who was standing next to him. Later, Napoleon would note this incident as the second time that his short stature had saved his life.

© Simon Tofield

8. Due to his common birth, Hideyoshi Toyotomi never took the title of *shogun*.

   ❑ True   ❑ False

9. Nicolas Soult, once one of Napoleon's most trusted marshals, attended the coronation of Queen Victoria.

   ❑ True   ❑ False

10. French general Maurice Gustav Gamelin was tried and executed for his part in the failure to stop the German invasion of France in 1940.

   ❑ True   ❑ False

ANSWERS

QUIZ 30 GENERAL
1)b 2)b 3)b 4)d 5)c 6)a 7)c 8)a 9)c 10)b

QUIZ 31 GENERAL
1) False. Merrill enlisted in the army in 1922, reaching the rank of sergeant before gaining entry to West Point. He graduated in 1929
2) False
3) True. Although since they could not distinguish enemy aircraft from Allied aircraft the practice was soon abandoned
4) False. Felix Zollicoffer from Tennessee held the rank of brigadier general when he was killed at the battle of Mill Springs in 1862
5) True
6) True
7) True
8) False. The French can join the Foreign Legion, but must do so under an assumed name and nationality
9) True
10) True

QUIZ 32 AIR WAR
1)b 2)d 3)c 4)b 5)c 6)b 7)d 8)d 9)a 10)d

QUIZ 33 GENERAL
1)c 2)c 3)b 4)b 5)a 6)c 7)a 8)a 9)c 10)d

QUIZ 34 GENERAL
1) Little Bighorn
2) The shin
3) Lützen
4) Shiroyama
5) Sergeant First Class
6) Cedar Mountain
7) Mikhail Kalashnikov
8) 24
9) 12
10) 10

QUIZ 35 THE PENINSULAR WAR
1)b 2)c 3)c 4)d 5)c 6)b 7)d 8)a 9)b 10)d

QUIZ 36 GENERAL
1)c 2)d 3)b 4)a 5)c 6)d 7)b 8)c 9)d 10)d

QUIZ 37 GENERAL

1) The English
2) Captain Thomas Hardy
3) The B-25 Mitchell
4) Britain
5) An early term for flintlock
6) Ali Pasha
7) Mark Antony
8) 70
9) "…the six hundred"
10) George Armstrong Custer

QUIZ 38 SPIES, CODEBREAKERS, AND ASSASSINS

1)b 2)c 3)c 4)b 5)a 6)c 7)b 8)c 9)d 10)a

QUIZ 39 GENERAL

1)a 2)a 3)b 4)b 5)d 6)c 7)a 8)c 9)b 10)b

QUIZ 40 GENERAL

1) True. Churchill was captured while serving as a journalist for the London *Morning Post*
2) True
3) True. He died in a plane crash with a group of Americans. The unidentified remains of all of the crew and passengers are buried together
4) False. He was the first lieutenant
5) False. Despite being momentarily cut off from his main army, Charles XII survived and even won the battle
6) True. Although the business venture proved a failure
7) True
8) False. He was a major slave owner
9) False. He made five unsuccessful attempts
10) True. According to the terms of the Antarctic Treaty

QUIZ 41 THE HUNDRED YEARS' WAR

1)d 2)a 3)d 4)c 5)d 6)b 7)a 8)c 9)d 10)c

QUIZ 42 GENERAL

1)b 2)d 3)c 4)c 5)a 6)d 7)c 8)d 9)a 10)c

QUIZ 43 GENERAL

1) St Benedict
2) Nicolas Soult
3) Radio Detecting and Ranging
4) King Macbeth

5) The Romans
6) Osman Digna
7) Operation *Thunderbolt*. It was renamed after Lieutenant Colonel Yonatan
   Netanyahu who was killed during the mission
8) Canister Smoke or ortho-chlorobenzylmalononitrile
9) Hastings, 1066
10) 1864

QUIZ 44 THE COLD WAR
1)b 2)b 3)a 4)c 5)d 6)d 7)a 8)b 9)b 10)d

THE GIANT AND THE DWARF.

"BRAVO, MY LITTLE FELLOW! YOU SHALL DO ALL THE FIGHTING, AND WE'LL DIVIDE THE GLORY!"

QUIZ 45 GENERAL
1)a 2)d 3)c 4)d 5)b 6)c 7)c 8)b 9)d 10)a

QUIZ 46 GENERAL
1) False. Three "Scud" missiles were fired by Egypt during the October War of 1973. However, they were so badly off target that the Israelis never realized they had been fired
2) True
3) True. The last Moorish stronghold of Granada fell in 1492. Columbus set sail in August of the same year
4) False. *Ronin* was the term given to a samurai without a master. Although some *ronin* became mercenaries, the majority became farmers or townspeople
5) False. However, the airship was involved in reconnaissance operations against the British radar stations in 1939 just before the outbreak of the war
6) False. The same story is also sometimes applied to Frederick the Great, but the true origins of cuff buttons predates them both and is unknown
7) False. Five British officers survived, but only one of these, Lieutenant Curling, was on the frontline
8) True
9) True. Timur was shot in the right leg and the right arm by arrows, both of which caused permanent damage
10) True

QUIZ 47 BIG GUNS
1)a 2)d 3)a 4)d 5)b 6)b 7)a 8)c 9)d 10)b

QUIZ 48 GENERAL
1)d 2)d 3)b 4)c 5)d 6)b 7)a 8)c 9)b 10)d

QUIZ 49 GENERAL
1) Iznik, Turkey
2) *Market Garden*
3) Kallinikos
4) James Monroe
5) A rock
6) War of the Triple Alliance
7) USS *Nautilus*
8) *Pezetaeri*
9) Rainbow Warrior
10) Hornet, will also accept Super Hornet

QUIZ 50 PUNIC WARS
1)d 2)b 3)c 4)b 5)c 6)d 7)c 8)c 9)c 10)d

QUIZ 51 GENERAL
1)b 2)a 3)d 4)a 5)d 6)a 7)c 8)c 9)c 10)b

QUIZ 52 GENERAL
1) False
2) True
3) True
4) True
5) False. However, his contemporary George Marshall did so
6) True
7) True. It was called Operation *Dirty Trick*
8) False. Thousands were killed
9) False. It was the American B-50 "Lucky Lady II" in 1949
10) True

QUIZ 53 WAR IN THE PACIFIC
1)d 2)b 3)b 4)d 5)c 6)c 7)c 8)a 9)d 10)b

QUIZ 54 GENERAL
1)d 2)d 3)b 4)a 5)c 6)b 7)c 8)a 9)c 10)a

QUIZ 55 GENERAL
1) True
2) False, but it was close
3) True
4) True
5) True
6) True
7) False. Over 500 Americans and over 2,000 Japanese were killed in the fighting for the island of Attu
8) False. Three members of the Ceylonese Garrison Artillery were hanged after leading an attack against their British officers
9) False. Around 100,000 fought, but there were only about 10,000 combined casualties
10) True. That day saw the battle of Antietam, with 23,000 casualties

QUIZ 56 VICTORIA'S WARS
1)b 2)b 3)a 4)c 5)c 6)b 7)a 8)c 9)c 10)c

QUIZ 57 GENERAL
1)d 2)b 3)d 4)b 5)a 6)a 7)d 8)c 9)c 10)b

QUIZ 58 GENERAL
1) Hannibal Hamlin
2) Jan Zizka

3) King's Mountain
4) Antoine Henri de Jomini
5) Nicaragua
6) USS *Vesuvius*
7) The Ancient and Honorable Artillery Company of Massachusetts, which now serves as the Honor Guard to the Governor
8) 1955
9) Alexander the Great. Philip of Macedon is also acceptable. He invented the portable artillery, though there is no proof he used it in battle
10) Horsa

QUIZ 59 GENERAL
1)b 2)b 3)c 4)c 5)d 6)b 7)d 8)a 9)a 10)c

QUIZ 60 GENERAL
1) The Japanese
2) Nathan Bedford Forrest
3) Field Marshal Wilhelm Keitel
4) George Washington
5) General Vo Nguyen Giap
6) Stephen Crane
7) The Japanese attack on Pearl Harbor
8) Gonzalo de Córdoba
9) Herrings, 1429
10) Sir Basil Henry Liddell-Hart

QUIZ 61 US PRESIDENTS
1)c 2)a 3)d 4)c 5)d 6)c 7)b 8)d 9)c 10)b

QUIZ 62 GENERAL
1)a 2)b 3)d 4)c 5)d 6)c 7)d 8)c 9)b 10)a

QUIZ 63 GENERAL
1) False. They sailed to Scapa Flow
2) False. It did in 1918
3) False. He died in 1964 at the age of 94
4) True
5) True
6) True
7) False. He was an Apache, but never a chief
8) True. He adopted the title of *kampaku* instead
9) True
10) False. He was arrested and tried, but the case was later dropped

THREE-STAR GENERAL
KNOWLEDGE

QUIZ 64

THE EASTERN FRONT, MULTIPLE CHOICE

1. Which Soviet marshal took command of the Second Ukranian Front in 1943, leading it in the battle of Kursk?

   ❑ a. Vasily Sokolovsky
   ❑ b. Konstantin Rokossovsky
   ❑ c. Georgi Konstantinovich Zhukov
   ❑ d. Ivan Stepanovich Konev

2. What was the original name of Operation *Blue* (or *Case Blue*) before Hitler changed it?

   ❑ a. Operation *Siegfried*   ❑ b. Operation *Roland*
   ❑ c. Operation *Mojonir*   ❑ d. Operation *Woden*

3. The German 37mm antitank gun acquired what nickname after facing Soviet T-34 tanks?

   ❑ a. the can opener   ❑ d. the gag gun
   ❑ c. the pop gun   ❑ d. the door-knocker

4. What is the Russian term for a "penal battalion"?

   ❑ a. *raputitsa*   ❑ b. *nazad*
   ❑ c. *shtrafbat*   ❑ d. *bezdororzh'e*

5. Operation *Störfang* was a plan to capture which city?

   ❑ a. Sevastopol   ❑ b. Moscow
   ❑ c. Leningrad   ❑ d. Stalingrad

6. The Allies provided the Soviet Union with the greatest number of which type of aircraft during World War II?

☐ a. P-40 Warhawk   ☐ b. B-25 Mitchell

☐ c. P-39 Airacobra   ☐ d. Spitfire

7. Which Soviet city is commonly known as "Tankograd"?

☐ a. Nizhnyi Tagil   ☐ b. Chelyabinsk

☐ c. Kharhov   ☐ d. Gorki

8. Which of the following best describes the "Hiwis"?

☐ a. Soviet partisan fighters

☐ b. long-range Soviet scouts

☐ c. Soviet horse and mule handlers

☐ d. Soviets who volunteered to work for the German Army

9. Which order stated that Soviet soldiers who tried to surrender to the enemy should be executed?

☐ a. No. 250   ☐ b. No. 270

☐ c. No. 310   ☐ d. No. 420

10. The Soviet battleship *Marat* is better known by which Russian name?

☐ a. *Karl Marx*   ☐ b. *Oktyabrskaya Revolutsia*

☐ c. *Petropavlovsk*   ☐ d. *Volodarski*

DIFFICULT

The great secret of battle is to have reserve.
The Duke of Wellington

QUIZ 65
GENERAL, MULTIPLE CHOICE

1. Which of the following is NOT a version of the Heckler
   & Koch G3 battle rifle?

   ❏ a. AG–3   ❏ b. Ak 4
   ❏ c. AG–3F1   ❏ d. LR–308

2. What is the regimental motto of the Black Watch?

   ❏ a. No man provokes me with impunity
   ❏ b. Death before dishonour
   ❏ c. Faithful and prepared
   ❏ d. I serve

3. Which South American country took on Britain and France in
   the 1845 battle of Obligado?

   ❏ a. Paraguay   ❏ b. Argentina
   ❏ c. Uruguay   ❏ d. Chile

4. Who was the last surviving person to have held the rank
   of general during the American Civil War?

   ❏ a. William Montgomery Gardner
   ❏ b. William Andrew Quarles
   ❏ c. Adelbert Ames
   ❏ d. James Alexander Walker

Aim for their shoelaces!
Oliver Cromwell

5. What was the name of Admiral John Byng's last flagship, which also served as the site of his execution in 1757?

    ❑ a. HMS *Victory*   ❑ b. HMS *Monarch*
    ❑ c. HMS *Indefatigable* ❑ d. HMS *Lion*

6. The 1353 battle of Yawata occurred in which country?

    ❑ a. China   ❑ b. Vietnam
    ❑ c. Japan   ❑ d. Burma

7. "Blackwater" is another name for which famous Irish battle?

    ❑ a. the Boyne   ❑ b. Yellow Ford
    ❑ c. Aughrim   ❑ d. Clontarf

8. Who played Lieutenent John Chard in the 1964 film *Zulu*?

    ❑ a. Stanley Baker   ❑ d. Michael Caine
    ❑ c. Jack Hawkins   ❑ d. James Booth

9. In 1677, the Danish under Christian V lost the battle of Landskrona to forces from which nation?

    ❑ a. Finland   ❑ b. Norway
    ❑ c. Germany   ❑ d. Sweden

10. The "first dog watch" is between which hours?

    ❑ a. 1600hrs and 1800hrs   ❑ b. 1800hrs and 2000hrs
    ❑ c. 2000hrs and 2200hrs   ❑ d. 2200hrs and 2400hrs

Come on you sons of bitches. Do you want to live forever?
Sergeant Dan Daly

GENERAL, SHORT ANSWER

1. Which Union general did Robert E. Lee label "a miscreant"?

. . . .

2. In 1798, the French Army occupied Rome, capturing which Pope?

. . . .

© Stars & Stripes

"Able Fox Five to Able Fox. I got a target, but ya gotta be patient."

3. How many British soldiers survived the Cawnpore Massacre in 1857?

. . . .

4. Who led the Dutch fleet to victory over the Spanish at the battle of the Downs in October 1639?

. . . .

5. What was the name of the Greek who betrayed the Spartans at Thermopylae?

. . . .

6. What was the first hot-air balloon to be deployed in battle?

. . . .

7. What was the first German city captured by the Allies during World War II?

. . . .

8. What were the names of Hannibal Barca's brothers?

. . . .

9. How many countries made up the "Anzus Pact"?

. . . .

10. The battle of Podol, fought on June 26, 1866, was part of which conflict?

. . . .

We do not believe that the aeroplane will ever take the place of the dirigible balloon...
Brigadier General James Allen, Head of the US Signal Corps

QUIZ 67

NATIVE AMERICAN WARS, MULTIPLE CHOICE

1. What was the last battle of the 1832 Black Hawk War?

   ❏ a. Stillman's Run   ❏ b. Buffalo Grove
   ❏ c. Waddams Grove   ❏ d. Bad Axe River

2. Which Native American chief was labelled the "Red Napoleon" by the American press?

   ❏ a. Chief Joseph   ❏ b. Sitting Bull
   ❏ c. Geronimo   ❏ d. Crazy Horse

3. In 1791, the Maumee Indians nearly wiped out the entire US Army under the command of Arthur St Clair in which present-day state?

   ❏ a. Pennsylvania   ❏ b. Ohio
   ❏ c. Michigan   ❏ d. Missouri

4. In the 1867 "Wagon Box Fight," Captain James Powell and just over 30 soldiers held off over 1,500 Indian warriors under which leader?

   ❏ a. Crazy Horse   ❏ b. Red Cloud
   ❏ c. Chief Joseph   ❏ d. Running Deer

5. The 1872–73 "Lava Beds War" is better known as which conflict?

   ❏ a. Nez Percé War   ❏ b. Bannock War
   ❏ c. Modoc War   ❏ d. Apache War

6. Which of the following battles was NOT a part of the Apache Wars?

☐ a. Apache Pass ☐ b. Big Bug
☐ c. Florida Mountains ☐ d. Broken Knife

7. In which American colony was the 1636 Pequot War fought?

☐ a. New York ☐ b. Connecticut
☐ c. Delaware ☐ d. Maryland

8. Which Native American was killed during an attempted arrest?

☐ a. Chief Joseph ☐ b. Sitting Bull
☐ c. Geronimo ☐ d. Red Cloud

9. Which year saw the last major Indian conflict and the battle of Wounded Knee?

☐ a. 1890 ☐ b. 1898
☐ c. 1901 ☐ d. 1906

10. Which of the following was an actual battle fought between the Native Americans and the US Cavalry?

☐ a. Red Dump Mountain ☐ b. Sitting Deer Stand
☐ c. Blackbird Drop ☐ d. Crazy Woman Fork

QUIZ 68
GENERAL, MULTIPLE CHOICE

1. In 1387 the naval forces of Richard II defeated a combined Franco-Castilian invasion force in the sea near which English town?

   ❏ a. Hastings   ❏ b. Hythe
   ❏ c. Margate   ❏ d. Dover

2. Which Eastern Roman Emperor led his soldiers to victory at the battle of Nineveh in AD 627?

   ❏ a. Constantine III   ❏ b. Phocas
   ❏ c. Heraklonas   ❏ d. Heraclius

3. Which Confederate general was defeated at the 1861 battle of Rich Mountain and then died soon after in a cavalry skirmish?

   ❏ a. Robert Garnett   ❏ b. Sterling Price
   ❏ c. Richard Taylor   ❏ d. Thomas Hindman

4. "Grog" was named after which British admiral?

   ❏ a. Arthur Champernowne   ❏ b. David Beatty
   ❏ c. Edward Vernon   ❏ d. Thomas Cochrane

5. Richard Neville, Earl of Warwick died in which 1471 battle of the Wars of the Roses?

   ❏ a. Barnet   ❏ b. Tewskesbury
   ❏ c. Losecote Field   ❏ d. Bosworth

6. In which plane did Chuck Yeager become the first man to officially break the sound barrier?

   ❑ a. XP-86 Sabre   ❑ b. Bell XS-1
   ❑ c. YF-100 Sub-Sabre   ❑ d. Douglas DC-8

7. Which son of Emperor Frederick II was killed in the 1266 battle of Benevento?

   ❑ a. Henry   ❑ b. Jordan
   ❑ c. Conrad   ❑ d. Manfred

8. How many enemy vessels did British admiral Lord Howe capture or sink on the "Glorious First of June" 1794?

   ❑ a. 4   ❑ b. 7
   ❑ c. 10   ❑ d. 12

9. The term "Chetniks" refers to guerrilla units from which state?

   ❑ a. Serbia   ❑ d. Czechoslavakia
   ❑ c. Greece   ❑ d. Romania

10. Which year saw the signing of the first Geneva Convention, which set out rules for the treatment of wounded soldiers on the battlefield?

    ❑ a. 1832   ❑ b. 1864
    ❑ c. 1877   ❑ d. 1886

Marches are war.
Napoleon Bonaparte

GENERAL, TRUE OR FALSE

1. "The Pacification of Berwick" ended the Second Bishops' War in 1640.
   ❑ True   ❑ False

2. There is a statue honoring General James Longstreet on the Gettysburg battlefield.
   ❑ True   ❑ False

3. During the 1914 battle of the Marne, the French used nearly 600 taxis to move reinforcements to the battlefield.
   ❑ True   ❑ False

4. Mildred E. Sisk, better known as "Axis Sally" was arrested after World War II and sentenced to life in a US prison.
   ❑ True   ❑ False

5. During World War II, no Axis prisoners of war managed to escape from Canada and make it back to Germany.
   ❑ True   ❑ False

DID YOU KNOW?

From his position working in the German embassy in Japan, the Russian spy Richard Sorge discovered both the plan for the German invasion of the Soviet Union and the Japanese attack on Pearl Harbor. He passed both pieces of information along to Moscow, and in both cases the information was ignored. Sorge was discovered and arrested by the Japanese in 1941. After the Soviets turned down three offers by the Japanese to exchange Sorge for one of their own operatives, Sorge was hanged on November 7, 1944.

6. Confederate President Jefferson Davis was a veteran of the Mexican–American War.

   ❏ True   ❏ False

7. At the battle of Abu Klea in 1885, the British Gatling gun jammed, allowing one corner of their square formation to be broken.

   ❏ True   ❏ False

8. American general Mark Clark appeared on the cover of *Time* magazine on three occasions.

   ❏ True   ❏ False

9. Despite his victory over the Persians at the naval battle of Arginusae in 406 BC, the Athenian leader Thrasyllus was executed for not taking proper steps to rescue the survivors of disabled ships.

   ❏ True   ❏ False

10. The term "gung-ho" comes from the Chinese for "working together."

    ❏ True   ❏ False

Subaltern: 'Between ourselves, sir, there'll be trouble with this Territorial captain. He's insufferable.'
Major: 'What of it? They said that about me.'
Subaltern: 'Ah, yes sir. But you're a regular. That's different.'

HORATIO NELSON, MULTIPLE CHOICE

1. During the battle of Copenhagen Nelson ignored the order to retire, which was given by which British admiral?

   ❑ a. Lord Howe   ❑ b. James Gambier
   ❑ c. Matthew Henry Scott   ❑ d. Hyde Parker

2. How many French ships of the line did Nelson face at the 1798 battle of the Nile?

   ❑ a. 4   ❑ b. 7
   ❑ c. 11   ❑ d. 13

3. In which year did Nelson take command of HMS *Agamemnon*?

   ❑ a. 1793   ❑ b. 1795
   ❑ c. 1797   ❑ d. 1799

4. What was Nelson's flagship during the 1801 battle of Copenhagen?

   ❑ a. HMS *Defiance*   ❑ b. HMS *Elephant*
   ❑ c. HMS *Monarch*   ❑ d. HMS *Bellona*

Firstly you must always implicitly obey orders, without attempting to form any opinion of your own respecting their propriety. Secondly, you must consider every man your enemy who speaks ill of your king; and thirdly you must hate a Frenchman as you hate the devil.

Admiral Horatio Nelson

5. Which sultan awarded Nelson a *chelengk* to wear in his hat after his victory at the Nile?

 ❑ a. Mustafa IV   ❑ b. Mahmud II
 ❑ c. Selim III   ❑ d. Abd Ülmecid

6. Which ship did Nelson command during the 1797 battle of Cape St Vincent?

 ❑ a. HMS *Captain*   ❑ b. HMS *Diadem*
 ❑ c. HMS *Minerve*   ❑ d. HMS *Goliath*

7. How many brothers and sisters did Nelson have?

 ❑ a. 0   ❑ b. 4
 ❑ c. 7   ❑ d. 10

8. Where did Nelson lose his right arm?

 ❑ a. Calvi   ❑ b. Santa Cruz
 ❑ c. St Vincent   ❑ d. Aboukir Bay

9. At what age did Nelson join the Royal Navy?

 ❑ a. 9   ❑ b. 10
 ❑ c. 11   ❑ d. 12

10. On which island did Nelson meet his future wife, Frances Nisbet?

 ❑ a. Jamaica   ❑ b. Nevis
 ❑ c. Antigua   ❑ d. Tobago

QUIZ 71
GENERAL, MULTIPLE CHOICE

1. Dutch admiral Karel Doorman went down with his ship in which 1942 battle in the Pacific?

   ☐ a. Madoera Strait ☐ b. Palembang
   ☐ c. Lombok Strait ☐ d. Java Sea

2. Which nation first declared war in the Crimea in 1853?

   ☐ a. the Ottoman Empire ☐ b. Russia
   ☐ c. France ☐ d. Britain

3. Which Union general captured Roanoke Island in 1862?

   ☐ a. Ulysses S. Grant ☐ b. George Mead
   ☐ c. Ambrose E. Burnside ☐ d. Joseph Hooker

4. *Maskirovka* is the Russian word for what?

   ☐ a. cavalry ☐ b. submarine
   ☐ c. tracked vehicle ☐ d. camouflage

5. In which conflict did the British Army last use the heliograph for communication?

   ☐ a. Second Sudan War ☐ b. World War I
   ☐ c. Anglo–Irish War ☐ d. World War II

In wartime no soldier is free to say what he thinks; after a war no one cares what a soldier thinks.

General Sir Ian Hamilton

6. The American M–388 "nuclear bazooka" was named after which American folk hero?

    ❑ a. Jesse James   ❑ b. Davy Crockett
    ❑ c. Jim Bowie   ❑ d. Wyatt Earp

7. At which battle did Suleiman "the Magnificent" defeat and kill the Hungarian king Louis II?

    ❑ a. Mohács   ❑ b. Szigetvár
    ❑ c. Preveza   ❑ d. Lefkada

8. The 1926–29 Ogbuloko War took place in which African country?

    ❑ a. Congo   ❑ b. Sudan
    ❑ c. Tanzania   ❑ d. Nigeria

9. The *Sicarii*, who defied Rome during the Great Revolt in AD 66, were named after which type of weapon?

    ❑ a. dagger   ❑ b. garrotte
    ❑ c. double curved bow   ❑ d. short, heavy-bladed spear

10. Which country spends the highest percentage of its GDP on its military?

    ❑ a. Jordan   ❑ b. Oman
    ❑ c. Saudi Arabia   ❑ d. Israel

GENERAL, SHORT ANSWER

1. Name a battle from the Napoleonic Wars that begins with the letter "Z."

   . . . .

2. The 1702 "Affair of the Spanish Galleons" is also known as the battle of what?

   . . . .

" All we had to eat was live cartridges."

3. Which World War II US artillery piece was known as a "Long Tom"?

   . . . .

4. Which British military leader went on to found the Boy Scouts in 1907?

   . . . .

5. Which caused more civilian deaths, the dropping of the atomic bomb on Nagasaki or the firebombing of Dresden?

   . . . .

DIFFICULT

6. Who abdicated the throne of Poland in 1738, thus ending the War of Polish Succession?

   . . . .

7. What was the British Army's first breech-loading personal firearm?

   . . . .

8. What was the codename for the order to scuttle the U-boat fleet, issued by Admiral Dönitz in April 1945?

   . . . .

9. Did the Dutch ally themselves with the French or British in the 1704 naval battle of Malaga?

   . . . .

10. Major General Heinrich Kreipe was kidnapped from occupied Crete during which World War II British operation?

   . . . .

RUSSIAN AND SOVIET COMMANDERS, MULTIPLE CHOICE

1. How many Soviet marshals were "purged" by Stalin during the 1930s?

   ❏ a. 0   ❏ b. 1
   ❏ c. 2   ❏ d. 3

2. Which Soviet marshal of World War II was famous for his mahogany-handled revolvers?

   ❏ a. Ivan Stepanovich Konev
   ❏ b. Semyon Mikhailovich Budenny
   ❏ c. Georgi Konstantinovich Zhukov
   ❏ d. Kliment Voroshilov

3. Who replaced Marshal Zhukov as commander of all Soviet ground forces in 1946?

   ❏ a. Semyon Mikhailovich Budenny
   ❏ b. Victor Kulikov
   ❏ c. Vasily Sokolovsky
   ❏ d. Ivan Stepanovich Konev

4. Who led the Russian forces at the 1770 battle of Karkal, defeating a combined Turkish and Tartar army?

   ❏ a. Count Peter Rumiantsev
   ❏ b. Prince Mikhail Ilarionovich Kutuzov
   ❏ c. Alexander Suvarov
   ❏ d. Alexander Alexandrovich Prozorosky

5. Whose armor was Michael Brenk wearing when he was killed during the 1380 battle of Kulikovo Field?

❑ a. Grand Prince Ivan Kalita
❑ b. Grand Prince Dmitrii Ivanovich
❑ c. Prince Daniil of Galich
❑ d. Prince Andrej Yaroslavich

6. How old was Prince Mikhail Ilarionovich Kutuzov when he was first posted as a Corporal of Artillery?

❑ a. 12   ❑ b. 14
❑ c. 15   ❑ d. 16

7. Who replaced General Alexei Kuropatkin as commander of the Russian forces facing the Japanese after the 1905 battle of Mukden?

❑ a. Dmitry Miljutin
❑ b. Konstantin Petrovich Kaufman
❑ c. Mikhail Skobelev
❑ d. Nikolay Linevich

8. Who did Tsar Nicholas II appoint as Supreme Commander of the Armed Forces of Russia on August 2, 1914?

❑ a. Grand Duke Nicholas Nicholaevitch
❑ b. Pavel Rennenkampf
❑ c. Alexi Brusilov
❑ d. Alexander Samsonov

The plan was smooth on paper, only they forgot about the ravines.
Russian military proverb

9. Which of the following was NOT one of the rebel leaders who joined Ivan Isayevich Bolotnikov during his 1606 siege of Moscow?

☐ a. Grigory Sumbulov   ☐ b. Fyodor Mstislavsky

☐ c. Prokopy Lyapunov   ☐ d. Istoma Pashkov

10. Apart from Georgi Zhukov, who is the only person to be named a Hero of the Soviet Union on four separate occasions?

☐ a. Pavel Popvich   ☐ b. Ivan Kozhedub

☐ c. Aleksander Pokryshkin   ☐ d. Leon Brezhnev

© TopFoto

"I understand you've been riveting in your name and address."

GENERAL, MULTIPLE CHOICE

1. What is the Confederate name for the battle of Cedar Mountain?

   ❏ a. Bettle's Woods   ❏ b. Switchback Creek
   ❏ c. Slaughter's Mountain   ❏ d. Twin Pines

2. The 1806 British invasion of Buenos Aires was led by which admiral?

   ❏ a. Home Riggs Popham   ❏ b. Richard Howe
   ❏ c. John Jervis   ❏ d. William Hothan

3. In the history of the United States, only two men have achieved the rank of "General of the Armies." The first was George Washington, who was the other?

   ❏ a. Ulysses S. Grant   ❏ b. John J. Pershing
   ❏ c. Douglas MacArthur   ❏ d. Dwight D. Eisenhower

4. German admiral Maximilian von Spee went down with his ship in which 1914 naval battle?

   ❏ a. Coronel   ❏ b. Jutland
   ❏ c. the Falklands   ❏ d. Heligoland Bight

5. What was the real name of "Lord Haw-Haw," executed by the British for treason in 1946?

   ❏ a. Jonah Barrington   ❏ b. Bertie Wooster
   ❏ c. Norman Baillie-Stewart ❏ d. William Joyce

DIFFICULT

6. Which famous *landsknecht* led the German mercenary contingent at the battle of Stoke in 1487?

   ❏ a. Martin Schwartz ❏ b. Georg von Frundsberg
   ❏ c. Pier Gerlofs Donia ❏ d. Cesare Hercolani

7. In which year was barbed wire invented?

   ❏ a. 1868 ❏ b. 1887
   ❏ c. 1901 ❏ d. 1913

8. Who held military command over the Zulus during their great victory at Isandlwana?

   ❏ a. Cetshwayo ❏ b. Zibhebhu
   ❏ c. Ntshingwayo ❏ d. Dinuzulu

9. The German Tiger tank had how many road wheels?

   ❏ a. 16 ❏ b. 24
   ❏ c. 32 ❏ d. 48

10. The 1866 battle of Ridgeway (or Lime Ridge) was fought in which country?

   ❏ a. Australia ❏ b. New Zealand
   ❏ c. Canada ❏ d. the United States

Infantry is the queen of Battles.
General Sir William Napier

GENERAL, TRUE OR FALSE

1. Carl Gustav Emil Mannerheim fought in the Russian Army during the Russo–Japanese War.
    ❑ True   ❑ False

2. American fighter ace Eddie Rickenbacker served for part of World War I as the chauffeur for General Pershing.
    ❑ True   ❑ False

3. William Wallace was captured by the English in the aftermath of the 1298 battle of Falkirk.
    ❑ True   ❑ False

4. Simon Bolívar died of tuberculosis.
    ❑ True   ❑ False

5. Chain shot was used on the battlefield during the Thirty Years' War.
    ❑ True   ❑ False

6. The Napoleonic Wars saw the first ever use of a submarine in wartime.
    ❑ True   ❑ False

7. The Americans captured over 100 French naval vessels during the 1798–1800 Quasi-War with France.
    ❑ True   ❑ False

8. At the outbreak of World War I, Britain possessed nearly twice as many submarines as Germany.
    ❑ True   ❑ False

9. The US Army ceased using mules and pigeons in the same year.
    ❑ True   ❑ False

10. The Soviet Union has only ever launched one "super-carrier."
    ❑ True   ❑ False

DIFFICULT

QUIZ 76

THE THIRTY YEARS' WAR, MULTIPLE CHOICE

1. *Hackabells* was a term for cavalry from which nation?

   ❑ a. Sweden   ❑ b. Finland
   ❑ c. Norway   ❑ d. Denmark

2. What poundage were the regimental cannons used in the army of Gustavus Adolphus?

   ❑ a. 3   ❑ b. 4
   ❑ c. 6   ❑ d. 12

3. The Imperial Marshal Peter Melander was mortally wounded in which battle fought in 1648?

   ❑ a. Lens   ❑ b. Nördlingen
   ❑ c. Zusmarshausen   ❑ d. Oglio

4. Which nation was the first to impose "running the gauntlet" as a form of military punishment?

   ❑ a. Sweden   ❑ b. France
   ❑ c. Spain   ❑ d. Russia

5. The 1620 battle of Weisser Berg (White Hill) was fought for possession of which city?

   ❑ a. Salzburg   ❑ b. Prague
   ❑ c. Venice   ❑ d. Vienna

6. Along with France, which was the first country to sign the Treaty of Compiégne as an alliance against the Hapsburgs?

- ❑ a. England
- ❑ b. Sweden
- ❑ c. Denmark
- ❑ d. The Netherlands

7. In which year did Gustavus Adolphus capture Frankfurt?

- ❑ a. 1631
- ❑ b. 1633
- ❑ c. 1634
- ❑ d. 1637

8. To which military commander was the town of Breda surrendered in 1625?

- ❑ a. Maximilian, Elector of Bavaria
- ❑ b. Ambrosio Spinola, Marqués de Los Balbases
- ❑ c. Johannes Tserclaes, Count von Tilly
- ❑ d. Gaspar de Guzmán, Count-Duke of Olivares

9. Who commanded the left wing of the Imperial Army at the 1631 battle of Breitenfeld?

- ❑ a. Count Andreas Schlick
- ❑ b. Charles Bucquoi
- ❑ c. Gottfried Pappenheim
- ❑ d. Johan Tserclaes, Count von Tilly

10. Baron Franz von Mercy was killed in 1645 at which battle?

- ❑ a. Mergentheim
- ❑ b. Jankau
- ❑ c. Lens
- ❑ d. Nördlingen

The more you hurt the enemy, the less he will hurt you.
Admiral David Farragut

GENERAL, MULTIPLE CHOICE

1. Which nation currently assumes the responsibility for the military defense of the island of Aruba?

   ❑ a. the United States   ❑ b. Great Britain
   ❑ c. France   ❑ d. the Netherlands

2. Santa Anna was captured by the Texans after which battle?

   ❑ a. Gonzales   ❑ b. La Bahia
   ❑ c. San Jacinto   ❑ d. San Antonio

3. Of the following countries, which provided the most volunteers for the International Brigades during the Spanish Civil War?

   ❑ a. Belgium   ❑ b. Poland
   ❑ c. the United States   ❑ d. Italy

4. Which one of the following states was never a member of the League of Cambrai?

   ❑ a. France
   ❑ b. the Papal States
   ❑ c. the Holy Roman Empire
   ❑ d. the Republic of Venice

5. How many rounds did the Le Mat "Grape Shot Revolver" hold in its cylinder?

   ❑ a. 6   ❑ b. 7
   ❑ c. 8   ❑ d. 9

6. Who led the Spaniards to defeat against the Muslims at the battle of Alarcos in 1195?

☐ a. Alfonso V
☐ b. Alfonso VI
☐ c. Alfonso VII
☐ d. Alfonso VIII

© Simon Tofield

7. *Bluebird*, *Dove*, and *Canary* were airborne missions during which operation?

☐ a. *Overlord* ☐ b. *Dragoon*
☐ c. *Market Garden* ☐ d. *Shingle*

8. Which battle, fought on September 13–14, 1515, was labelled "The Battle of Giants" by Marshal Trivulzio?

☐ a. Marignano ☐ b. Novara
☐ c. Magenta ☐ d. Venice

9. What was the birth name of Ulysses Simpson Grant?

☐ a. Hiram Simpson Grant ☐ b. Hiram Ulysses Grant
☐ c. Ezekiel Hiram Grant ☐ d. Ezekiel Simpson Grant

10. What was the last battle between Cnut and Edmund Ironsides?

☐ a. Sherstone ☐ b. Ashdown
☐ c. Pen Selwood ☐ d. Assandun

Our army is composed of the scum of the earth – the mere scum of the earth.
The Duke of Wellington

QUIZ 78
GENERAL, SHORT ANSWER

1. Who said, "Britain is not worth an old shoe"?

   ....

2. Which war began because of the "Marco Polo Bridge Incident"?

   ....

3. Who was the first member of the Imperial Order of the Crescent, the Ottoman chivalric order?

   ....

4. Which battle in 1868 forced Queen Isabel II of Spain to flee to France?

. . . .

5. Who was the British "Secretary of State of the American Department" during the American Revolution?

. . . .

6. Which World War I German commander said, "black or white, the superior man will always outwit the inferior"?

. . . .

7. Who won the 1476 battle of Morat, the Swiss or the Burgundians?

. . . .

8. *Shogun* Oda Nobunaga committed suicide after being surrounded by the forces of which of his rebellious generals?

. . . .

9. Which son of James II of England led the French forces at the 1707 battle of Almansa?

. . . .

10. Which US general was sometimes known as "Old fuss and feathers"?

. . . .

If I had worried about flanks, I could never have fought the war.
General George S. Patton

QUIZ 79

WORLD WAR II IN ITALY, MULTIPLE CHOICE

1. On which date did the Allies capture Rome?

   ☐ a. June 2, 1944   ☐ b. June 3, 1944
   ☐ c. June 4, 1944   ☐ d. June 5, 1944

2. Who held command over the Italian forces stationed in Sicily during Operation *Husky*?

   ☐ a. Alfredo Fedele   ☐ b. Gualtiero Frattali
   ☐ c. Alfredo Guzzoni   ☐ d. Giuseppe Vallerini

3. How many battleships of the *Vittorio Veneto* (or *Littorio*) class did Italy manage to complete?

   ☐ a. 0   ☐ b. 1
   ☐ c. 2   ☐ d. 3

4. What was the German name for the K5E railroad gun known to the Americans as "Anzio Annie"?

   ☐ a. Hindenburg   ☐ d. Leopold
   ☐ c. Siegfried   ☐ d. Blücher

5. Who was appointed Supreme Allied Commander Mediterranean after the departure of Dwight D. Eisenhower?

   ☐ a. Oliver Leese   ☐ b. Henry Maitland Wilson
   ☐ c. Mark Clark   ☐ d. Harold Alexander

6. Who among the following was NOT a Corps commander in the US Fifth Army in Italy?

   ❑ a. Geoffrey Keyes   ❑ b. John P. Lucas
   ❑ c. Alphonse Juin   ❑ d. Wladyslaw Anders

7. The town of Cassino sits next to which river?

   ❑ a. Tiber   ❑ b. Rapido
   ❑ c. Garigliano   ❑ d. Sangro

8. Troops from which Allied nation first raised a flag over the ruins of the Cassino monastery on May 18, 1944?

   ❑ a. the United States   ❑ b. Great Britain
   ❑ c. France   ❑ d. Poland

9. What was the codename of the 1943 Casablanca conference during which the Allies agreed to invade Sicily?

   ❑ a. *Tinder*   ❑ b. *Circle*
   ❑ c. *Symbol*   ❑ d. *Silver*

10. On which date was the armistice between Italy and the Allies announced?

   ❑ a. September 1, 1943   ❑ b. September 8, 1943
   ❑ c. September 15, 1943   ❑ d. September 22, 1943

We will either find a way, or make one.
Hannibal

GENERAL, MULTIPLE CHOICE

1. Suleiman the Magnificent died during the siege of which fortress?

   ❑ a. Malta
   ❑ b. Rhodes
   ❑ c. Szigetvar
   ❑ d. Peterwardein

DIFFICULT

2. Which treaty saw the end of the 1904–05 Russo–Japanese War?

   ❑ a. Treaty of Prague
   ❑ b. Treaty of Pearl Harbor
   ❑ c. Treaty of Portsmouth
   ❑ d. Treaty of Paris

3. Which year saw the final evacuation of American troops from Germany after World War I?

   ❑ a. 1918
   ❑ b. 1919
   ❑ c. 1923
   ❑ d. 1927

4. Which European nation suffered the most casualties fighting in Sumatra in the 18th and 19th centuries?

   ❑ a. Great Britain
   ❑ b. France
   ❑ c. the Netherlands
   ❑ d. Germany

5. Which of these Viking leaders was born first?

   ❑ a. Gorm
   ❑ b. Harald Bluetooth
   ❑ c. Sweyn Forkbeard
   ❑ d. Canute

6. What kind of soldier was a *genitour*?

   ❑ a. light infantryman
   ❑ b. heavy infantryman
   ❑ c. light cavalryman
   ❑ d. heavy cavalryman

7. Which European power eventually intervened in the 1891–93 Wahehe War?

  ❑ a. Britain   ❑ b. Germany
  ❑ c. Belgium   ❑ d. Italy

8. During the 1859 war between Austria and the allies France and Piedmont, which city was not part of the famous fortified "Quadrilateral"?

  ❑ a. Mantua   ❑ b. Milan
  ❑ c. Pescheira   ❑ d. Verona

9. Which country went to war with Tran Ninn in 1651?

  ❑ a. Cambodia   ❑ b. Malaya
  ❑ c. Indonesia   ❑ d. Laos

10. Which of the following was the son of Charlemagne?

  ❑ a. Louis the German ❑ b. Charles the Bald
  ❑ c. Lothair   ❑ d. Louis the Pius

Order a naval rating to "secure the house" and he'll enter it, close all the doors and windows, and throw a line over the roof and lash it down. Order an infantryman to "secure the house" and he'll enter it, shoot anything that moves and dig a trench around it. Order an airman to "secure the house" and he'll stroll down to the local estate agent and take out a seven-year lease on it.

British military adage

GENERAL, TRUE OR FALSE

1. The US Marine Corps has several fighter wings equipped with A-10 Thunderbolt IIs.

   ❑ True　　　❑ False

2. Ferdinand Foch, who would later lead the Allied forces on the Western Front in 1918, was decorated for valor during the Franco-Prussian War.

   ❑ True　　　❑ False

© Stars & Stripes

"I just ain't worth a damn in the morning without a hot cup of coffee."

3. Vo Nguyen Giap fought under Mao as a guerrilla in China during World War II.

❑ True   ❑ False

4. General Winfield Scott ran for President of the United States in 1852.

❑ True   ❑ False

5. Stephen Decatur once shot the "Jersey Devil" with a cannon.

❑ True   ❑ False

6. No former President or Vice-President of the United States fought for the Confederacy.

❑ True   ❑ False

7. George S. Patton won an Olympic medal.

❑ True   ❑ False

8. The armies of Gustavus Adolphus had ceased using leather cannons by 1630.

❑ True   ❑ False

9. The term "Doughboy" for a US soldier predates World War I.

❑ True   ❑ False

10. Jean Le Meingre "Boucicaut" was captured by the English at Agincourt, but was NOT killed when Henry ordered the execution of the prisoners.

❑ True   ❑ False

There is nothing certain about war except that one side won't win.
General Sir Ian Hamilton

THE VIETNAM WAR, MULTIPLE CHOICE

1. Which country did NOT send combat troops to support the American efforts in Vietnam?

   ❑ a. New Zealand ❑ b. United Kingdom
   ❑ c. Thailand ❑ d. Republic of Korea

2. In which year was the battle of Ap Bac fought?

   ❑ a. 1963 ❑ b. 1967
   ❑ c. 1970 ❑ d. 1973

3. What name was given to the initial American landing zone during the 1965 battle of the Ia Drang Valley?

   ❑ a. Albany ❑ b. X-Ray
   ❑ c. Spike ❑ d. Utah

4. On which day of 1968 did the Viet Cong and NVA forces launch the Tet Offensive?

   ❑ a. January 15 ❑ b. January 30
   ❑ c. February 15 ❑ d. February 28

5. Which Vietnamese general held command of the 35 battalions of NVA and Viet Cong who attacked Saigon during the Tet Offensive?

   ❑ a. Hoàng Van Thài ❑ b. Tràn Van Trà
   ❑ c. Võ Chí Công ❑ d. Pham Hùng

DIFFICULT

6. What was the operational name of the aerial counter-strike against NVA and Viet Cong forces assaulting the Marine base at Khe Sanh in 1967?

   ❑ a. *Mississippi*
   ❑ b. *Colorado*
   ❑ c. *Yellow Stone*
   ❑ d. *Niagara*

7. Who succeeded General William Westmoreland as Commander of US Forces in South Vietnam?

   ❑ a. Maxwell Taylor
   ❑ b. Frederick Wayand
   ❑ c. Earl Wheeler
   ❑ d. Creighton Abrams

8. Which of the following best describes "The Menu Series"?

   ❑ a. CIA operatives implanted in remote villages
   ❑ b. targeted assassination of Viet Cong leaders
   ❑ c. bombing of communist bases in Cambodia
   ❑ d. the secret evacuation of US personnel from Vietnam

9. Which hill would later become known as "Hamburger Hill"?

   ❑ a. Hill 812
   ❑ b. Hill 872
   ❑ c. Hill 912
   ❑ d. Hill 937

10. Who wrote the anti-war song, "Fortunate Son"?

   ❑ a. Neil Young
   ❑ b. Stephen Stills
   ❑ c. John Fogerty
   ❑ d. Bruce Springsteen

GENERAL, MULTIPLE CHOICE

1. What was the highest rank obtained by Robert Rogers in the British Army?

    ❑ a. captain   ❑ b. major
    ❑ c. colonel   ❑ d. general

2. A Galloglass *corrughadh* or "battle" was made up of smaller units called what?

    ❑ a. lances   ❑ b. spars
    ❑ c. brothers   ❑ d. squares

3. Who was the last Confederate Secretary of War?

    ❑ a. Leroy Walker   ❑ b. Juday Benjamin
    ❑ c. John Breckinridge   ❑ d. James Seddon

4. Which of the following American divisions that fought in Europe in World War II wore a rainbow on its divisional patch?

    ❑ a. 26th   ❑ b. 42nd
    ❑ c. 69th   ❑ d. 71st

DIFFICULT

> *A man does not get himself killed for a halfpence a day or for a petty distinction. You must speak to the soul to electrify him.*
> Napoleon Bonaparte

5. What term was used to describe the Seleucid soldiers whose function was to protect the legs of an elephant?

☐ a. *keddah*   ☐ b. *jingall*
☐ c. *mahout*   ☐ d. *stiphos*

6. Approximately how many Medals of Honor were awarded for actions during World War I?

☐ a. 50   ☐ b. 120
☐ c. 180   ☐ d. 250

7. Which of Charles II's loyal commanders was mortally wounded at the 1652 battle of Worcester?

☐ a. Lord Derby   ☐ b. Lord Lauderdale
☐ c. Lord Kenmure   ☐ d. the Duke of Hamilton

8. Who led the Poles to victory at the battle of Bug River in 1018?

☐ a. Boleslav the Brave   ☐ b. Mieszko II Lambert
☐ c. Bezprym   ☐ d. Otton

9. Who led the Brandenburgers during the 1679 battle of Splitter?

☐ a. Frederick William   ☐ b. George William
☐ c. Albert Frederick   ☐ d. John Sigismund

10. Which battle in the Jacobite Rebellion is also known as the battle of Gladsmuir?

☐ a. Prestonpans   ☐ b. Preston
☐ c. Culloden   ☐ d. Falkirk

QUIZ 84
GENERAL, SHORT ANSWER

1. Who was the youngest combat pilot in the US Navy in World War II?

. . . .

2. Which military leader during the French Revolution claimed victories at the 1797 battle of Rivoli?

. . . .

"I could swore a coupla Krauts wuz usin' that cow fer cover, Joe. Go wake up th' cooks . . ."

3. Who was victorious at the 1676 naval battle of Entholm, the Danes or the Swedes?

. . . .

4. Who raised and led the "Yorkshire Redcaps" during the 1639 Bishops' Wars?

. . . .

5. The Japanese term *Shinobi no mono* refers to what?

. . . .

6. Which hand did Roman legionaries use to salute?

. . . .

7. What is the first battle known to have been won by the decisive use of handheld firearms?

. . . .

8. Who designed the M1 carbine?

. . . .

9. What are the next four words after, "Once more unto the breach…"

. . . .

10. Which French artillerist officially separated artillery into three types: field, siege, and coastal?

. . . .

The man who is prepared has his battle half fought.
Miguel de Cervantes, *Don Quixote*

THE WAR FOR IRELAND, MULTIPLE CHOICE

1. Erskine Childers was executed by the Free State government in November 1922 for illegally owning a pistol that had been given to him as a gift by whom?

   ❑ a. Michael Collins ❑ b. Eamon de Valera
   ❑ c. Sir Roger Casement ❑ d. Tom Barry

2. On which date in 1920 did Tom Barry carry out his Kilmichael ambush?

   ❑ a. November 28 ❑ b. October 28
   ❑ c. September 28 ❑ d. August 28

3. Who commanded the Free State troops at the siege and capture of Kilkenny Castle?

   ❑ a. General Richard Mulcahy
   ❑ b. Colonel John Prout
   ❑ c. Lieutenant General J. J. O'Connell
   ❑ d. Major General James Dalton

4. Which vessel shelled the Citizens' Army headquarters at Liberty Hall in 1916?

   ❑ a. SS *Arvonia* ❑ b. SS *Lady Wicklow*
   ❑ c. SS *Alexandra* ❑ d. HMY *Helga*

5. The "Howth" rifles, named for the town into which they were smuggled, were predominately of what type?

   ❏ a. Lee Enfield
   ❏ b. Mauser
   ❏ c. Lebel
   ❏ d. Springfield

6. Marked by the relief of the Dublin Castle garrison by National Army troops, on what date did British rule in Ireland end?

   ❏ a. January 21, 1919
   ❏ b. July 11, 1921
   ❏ c. December 6, 1921
   ❏ d. January 16, 1922

7. What was the first unit to be formed as part of the National Army?

   ❏ a. the Dublin Guards
   ❏ b. the Civic Guards
   ❏ c. the Dublin Brigade
   ❏ d. the Eastern Division

8. Who remarked upon the rising tide of Republicanism that followed the Easter Rising with the line, "a terrible beauty is born"?

   ❏ a. T. S. Eliot
   ❏ b. W. B. Yeats
   ❏ c. Wilfred Owen
   ❏ d. Siegfried Sassoon

9. What was the name of Erskine Childers' yacht, in which he landed the Easter Rising rebels' principal arms supply at Howth?

   ❏ a. *Kelpie*
   ❏ b. *Asgard*
   ❏ c. *Gladiators*
   ❏ d. *Aud*

10. What was the full name of "The O'Rahilly"?

   ❏ a. Patrick Joseph O'Rahilly
   ❏ b. James Clarke O'Rahilly
   ❏ c. Tom James O'Rahilly
   ❏ d. Michael Joseph O'Rahilly

GENERAL, MULTIPLE CHOICE

1. Which Native American leader led a combined force of Sioux, Cheyenne, and Arapaho during the 1866 "Fetterman Massacre"?

   ❑ a. Crazy Horse   ❑ b. Geronimo
   ❑ c. Red Cloud   ❑ d. Cochise

DIFFICULT

2. Which 1870 battle of the Franco-Prussian War is also known as the battle of Vionville?

   ❑ a. Sedan   ❑ b. Gravelotte
   ❑ c. Mars-la-Tour   ❑ d. Metz

3. Which country first employed mustard gas as a weapon?

   ❑ a. Russia   ❑ b. France
   ❑ c. Italy   ❑ d. Germany

4. When Wellington formed his first cabinet in 1828, who took over his position as Commander-in-Chief of the Forces?

   ❑ a. William Carr Beresford
   ❑ b. Henry Hardinge
   ❑ c. Rowland Hill
   ❑ d. Prince George, Duke of Cambridge

5. Castillon, generally considered to be the last battle of the Hundred Years' War, was fought in which year?

   ❑ a. 1412   ❑ b. 1432
   ❑ c. 1444   ❑ d. 1453

6. What was the last ship commanded by Sir Richard Grenville?

☐ a. *Defiant*   ☐ b. *Revenge*
☐ c. *Falcon*   ☐ d. *Sparrowhawk*

7. Which Japanese general commanded the garrison of Iwo Jima during the American attack in 1945?

☐ a. Tadamichi Kuribayashi   ☐ b. Mutsumikichi Ryuko
☐ c. Count Seiki Terauchi   ☐ d. Yoji Wachi

8. What was the first battle of the Wars of the Roses?

☐ a. Northampton   ☐ b. St Albans
☐ c. Towton   ☐ d. Bosworth

9. Which of the following is NOT a school for military cadets?

☐ a. The Citadel   ☐ b. St-Cyr
☐ c. Maria Theresa Akademie   ☐ d. Pooleside

10. What was the real name of "General Bór," commander of the Polish Underground Army?

☐ a. Tadeusz Komorowski
☐ b. Michal Karaszewicz-Tokarzewski
☐ c. Stefan Rowecki
☐ d. Leopold Okulicki

Happy is that city which in time of peace prepares for war.
Inscription in the Armory of Venice

QUIZ 87
GENERAL, TRUE OR FALSE

1. John Wayne was turned down by the US Military Academy at West Point.
   ❑ True ❑ False

2. James Thomas Brudenell, 7th Earl of Cardigan, died in a duel arising from his conduct during the battle of Balaclava.
   ❑ True ❑ False

3. The term "commando" comes from the Boer War.
   ❑ True ❑ False

4. The United States awarded more medals for the 1984 invasion of Grenada than there were US soldiers who landed on the island.
   ❑ True ❑ False

5. Officially, no one in World War II was killed by a giant squid.
   ❑ True ❑ False

6. James Graham, 1st Marquis of Montrose, was a signatory of the Scottish Covenant.
   ❑ True ❑ False

7. During the 1942 battle of the Coral Sea, no surface vessel ever came within visual range of an enemy surface vessel.
   ❑ True ❑ False

8. At one point, General Nathaniel Greene lost four straight engagements in the southern campaign of the American Revolution.
   ❑ True ❑ False

Nothing so comforts the military mind as the maxims of a dead but great general.
Barbara W. Tuchman

DIFFICULT

9. Only four Nazis were tried for genocide at Nuremburg.
   ☐ True   ☐ False

10. John J. Pershing was promoted directly from captain to
    brigadier general.
    ☐ True   ☐ False

GENERAL, MULTIPLE CHOICE

1. In which battle of the War of the Austrian Succession was Louis-Joseph Montcalm wounded by five saber slashes before being captured?

   ☐ a. Lauffeld   ☐ b. Mollwitz

   ☐ c. Rocoux   ☐ d. Piacenza

2. What was the original numerical designation for the unit eventually named the 77th Foot, Montgomery's Highlanders?

   ☐ a. 61st   ☐ b. 62nd

   ☐ c. 63rd   ☐ d. 66th

3. Which battle, won by Simon Bolívar in 1824, was won completely by sword and lance?

   ☐ a. Cartagena   ☐ b. Carabobo

   ☐ c. Pichincha   ☐ d. Junin

4. Which of these admirals never used HMS *Victory* as his flagship?

   ☐ a. Charles Hardy

   ☐ b. Hyde Parker

   ☐ c. Benjamin Halowell Carew

   ☐ d. John Jervis

5. Prince Eugéne was a member of which order of knighthood?

   ☐ a. the Sacred Heart   ☐ b. the Golden Fleece

   ☐ c. the Sword Brethren   ☐ d. the Iron Cross

DIFFICULT

6. In 1853, Britain established a school of musketry in which seaside town?

   ❑ a. Folkestone   ❑ b. Seabrook
   ❑ c. Hythe   ❑ d. Sandgate

7. What was the operational name for the 1982 Israeli invasion of Lebanon?

   ❑ a. *Grapes of Wrath*   ❑ b. *Summer Rain*
   ❑ c. *Peace for Galilee*   ❑ d. *Spring of Youth*

8. Which woman's name did the Allies assign to the Japanese Nakajima B5N2 Type 97 horizontal bombers?

   ❑ a. Kate   ❑ b. Sue
   ❑ c. Dolly   ❑ d. Pam

9. On average, how many feet of a 21ft Swiss pike from the 15th century were taken up by the wooden shaft?

   ❑ a. 21   ❑ b. 20
   ❑ c. 18   ❑ d. 15

10. The 1547 battle of Pinkie Cleugh was fought over which Scottish river?

   ❑ a. Carron   ❑ b. Till
   ❑ c. Esk   ❑ d. Tweed

Nobody in the British Army ever reads a regulation or an order as if it were to be a guide for his conduct, or in any other manner than as an amusing novel.
The Duke of Wellington

GENERAL, SHORT ANSWER

1. Which two British monitors eventually managed to sink the German raider *Königsberg* in 1915?

. . . .

DIFFICULT

© Stars & Stripes

"Run it up th' mountain agin, Joe. It ain't hot enough."

2. Who was the primary author of *Truppenführung* (Unit Command), the German tactical manual published in two parts in 1932 and 1933?

....

3. Which Union general would later serve as an observer in the Franco-Prussian War before becoming General-in-Chief of the US Army?

....

4. Who was the first Supreme Military Commander of the Warsaw Pact?

....

5. Which of Gustavus Adolphus' field marshals is known as "the father of field artillery"?

....

6. Who commanded the "Legion of the United States" in 1792?

....

7. What was the name of the king's standard-bearer who was killed at the 1642 battle of Edgehill?

....

8. Which 1920 treaty secured the independence of Finland from Russia?

....

9. Who led the allied French and Bavarians in their defense of Dönauworth against the army of Marlborough in 1704?

....

10. What was the last name of "Vinegar Joe," the commander of US forces in the China-Burma-India theater in World War II?

....

QUIZ 90
DIXIE

1. Which Confederate regiment suffered the most casualties during a single battle when it fought on the field of Gettysburg?

   ❏ a. 16th South Carolina   ❏ b. 16th North Carolina
   ❏ c. 16th Virginia   ❏ d. 26th North Carolina

2. Who was the commanding officer of the infamous Andersonville prisoner of war camp?

   ❏ a. Jacob Skelly   ❏ b. Herman Nice
   ❏ c. Henry Wirz   ❏ d. Deacon John Jones

3. What is the full name of General D. H. Hill?

   ❏ a. David Henry Hill   ❏ b. Daniel Harvey Hill
   ❏ c. David Harvey Hill   ❏ d. Daniel Henry Hill

4. Which Confederate general was known for riding an ugly horse?

   ❏ a. Richard Ewell
   ❏ b. Ambrose Powell Hill
   ❏ c. James Longstreet
   ❏ d. Thomas J. "Stonewall" Jackson

5. In which year was General Robert E. Lee named General-in-Chief of the Confederate armies?

   ❏ a. 1865   ❏ b. 1864
   ❏ c. 1863   ❏ d. 1862

6. Jefferson Davis was Secretary of War under which US president?

   ❑ a. James Garfield   ❑ b. Chester Arthur
   ❑ c. James Buchanan   ❑ d. Franklin Pierce

7. After the sinking of CSS *Alabama*, Captain Raphael Simms was rescued by a yacht belonging to which nation?

   ❑ a. France   ❑ b. Great Britain
   ❑ c. the Netherlands   ❑ d. Sweden

8. What is the Confederate name for the battle of Stones River?

   ❑ a. Murfreesboro   ❑ b. Shiloh
   ❑ c. Hartsville   ❑ d. the Wilderness

9. According to Confederate general Wade Hampton, what was the best regiment in either army during the American Civil War?

   ❑ a. Hampton's Legion   ❑ b. Cobb's Legion Cavalry
   ❑ c. Jeff Davis Legion   ❑ d. 1st Virginia Cavalry

10. In 1864, General Jubal Early burned down the town of Chambersburg, Pennsylvania, in retaliation for the burning of which of the following by the Union Army?

   ❑ a. Richmond Capitol Building
   ❑ b. Atlanta Medical College
   ❑ c. Virginia Military Institute
   ❑ d. Robert E. Lee's house

To fight without a reserve is similar to playing cards without capital – sheer gambling. To trust to the cast of dice is not generalship.
Major General J. F. C. Fuller

GENERAL, MULTIPLE CHOICE

1. What was the last battle in which an English monarch led troops into battle?

   ❏ a. Fontenoy   ❏ b. Chotusitz
   ❏ c. Mollwitz   ❏ d. Dettingen

2. Out of Paraguay, Cuba, Oman, Finland, and Bolivia, how many declared war on Germany in World War II?

   ❏ a. 0   ❏ b. 2
   ❏ c. 4   ❏ d. 5

3. Which of these is another name for the Decelean War?

   ❏ a. the Archidamian War   ❏ b. the Sicilian Expedition
   ❏ c. the Crete War   ❏ d. the Ionian War

4. An accusation of what crime forced Robert Rogers to join the New Hampshire Volunteers in 1755?

   ❏ a. poaching   ❏ b. murder
   ❏ c. counterfeiting ❏ d. theft

5. Which regiment of the British Army was popularly known as the "Drogheda Light Horse"?

   ❏ a. 4th Royal Irish Dragoon Guards
   ❏ b. 18th Hussars
   ❏ c. 15th Hussars
   ❏ d. 3rd Light Dragoons

6. How many teeth were required for a US volunteer soldier in 1917?

   ❑ a. 0   ❑ b. 2
   ❑ c. 20   ❑ d. 30

7. Who did Clovis defeat at the battle of Soissons in 486?

   ❑ a. Gundomar   ❑ b. Gundobad
   ❑ c. Syagrius   ❑ d. Alaric II

8. The motto of which English regiment declares itself "Second to None"?

   ❑ a. the Parachute Regiment
   ❑ b. the Horse Guards
   ❑ c. the Coldstream Guards
   ❑ d. the Irish Guards

9. In which year did Chinese communist forces begin their "Long March"?

   ❑ a. 1927   ❑ b. 1929
   ❑ c. 1931   ❑ d. 1934

10. What was the only battlefield defeat in the career of Gonzalo de Córdoba?

    ❑ a. Seminara   ❑ b. Atella
    ❑ c. Cerignola   ❑ d. Cephalonia

A man-of-war is the best ambassador.
Oliver Cromwell

GENERAL, TRUE OR FALSE

1. The first recorded battle to involve an ironclad ship was fought in 1592.

   ❏ True   ❏ False

2. West Point was designed, and its construction overseen, by a German volunteer in the Continental Army.

   ❏ True   ❏ False

3. Jean Parisot de La Valette, Grand Master of the Order of the Hospital of St John of Jerusalem, spent nearly six years as a galley slave.

   ❏ True   ❏ False

4. For most of World War II, the United States produced no civilian automobiles.

   ❏ True   ❏ False

5. The 825 battle of Ellandune saw the West Saxons under Egbert defeat the Mercians under Beowulf.

   ❏ True   ❏ False

DIFFICULT

DID YOU KNOW?

Captain Michel Bacos was the pilot of Air France Flight 139 that was hijacked in 1976. After the plane touched down at Entebbe Airport in Uganda, many of the non-Jewish hostages were set free. Michel Bacos and the rest of the flight crew decided to stay with the remaining hostages and helped support them until they were eventually rescued by the Israeli Defense Force. For his heroic action, Air France suspended Michel Bacos.

6. Major General "Mad Anthony" Wayne had no military experience prior to the outbreak of the American Revolution.
   ❏ True   ❏ False

7. Most of the soldiers who fought as part of the Connaught Rangers during the Peninsular War were actually English.
   ❏ True   ❏ False

8. August Wilhelm Anton Gneisenau first fought in a battle during the American Revolution.
   ❏ True   ❏ False

9. Louis-Joseph Montcalm never held direct command of an army of more than 6,000 men.
   ❏ True   ❏ False

10. Despite losing nearly half of the Red Army during the German invasion, Soviet marshal Demyon Mikhailovich Budenny was named a hero of the Soviet Union.
    ❏ True   ❏ False

To astonish is to vanquish.
Field Marshal Prince Aleksandr V. Suvorov

NAPOLEON'S MARSHALS, MULTIPLE CHOICE

1. Which of Napoleon's marshals did Wellington claim kept him awake at night?

   ❏ a. Michel Ney ❏ b. Nicolas-Jean de Dieu Soult
   ❏ c. André Masséna ❏ d. Joachim Murat

2. When Napoleon left his army during the retreat from Moscow, whom did he leave in command?

   ❏ a. Joachim Murat ❏ b. Michel Ney
   ❏ c. Louis Davout ❏ d. Charles Oudinot

3. To which of his marshals did Napoleon assign the defense of Paris during the Hundred Days?

   ❏ a. Charles Oudinot
   ❏ b. Laurent de Gouvion Saint-Cyr
   ❏ c. Fraçois Joseph Lefebvre
   ❏ d. Louis Davout

4. Before becoming a Marshal of France, which commander led the French Army in the capture of Zürich in 1802?

   ❏ a. Michel Ney
   ❏ b. Nicolas-Jean de Dieu Soult
   ❏ c. André Masséna
   ❏ d. Laurent de Gouvion Saint-Cyr

DIFFICULT

5. Which of Napoleon's marshals led the corps that stormed the bridge and castle of Ebersberg in 1809?

- ☐ a. Claude Victor
- ☐ b. Louis Davout
- ☐ c. André Masséna
- ☐ d. Laurent de Gouvion Saint-Cyr

6. Who led the French against the Spanish in the 1808 battle of Espinosa?

- ☐ a. Nicolas-Jean de Dieu Soult
- ☐ b. Laurent de Gouvion Saint-Cyr
- ☐ c. Claude Victor
- ☐ d. Joachim Murat

7. What was the official length of a marshal's baton?

- ☐ a. 30cm
- ☐ b. 50cm
- ☐ c. 70cm
- ☐ d. 90cm

8. Which of Napoleon's marshals was appointed leader of the Armée des Alpes on April 26, 1815 and led an invasion of Savoy?

- ☐ a. Louis-Gabriel Suchet, Duc d'Albufera
- ☐ b. Claude Victor-Perrin, Duc de Bellune
- ☐ c. Catherine-Dominique, Marquis de Périgon
- ☐ d. Prince Josef Anton Poniatowski

9. Which of Napoleon's marshals had previous experience as the Ambassador to the Ottoman Empire?

- ☐ a. Guillaume Marie Anne-Brune
- ☐ b. Jean-Baptiste Bessiéres, Duc d'Istrie
- ☐ c. Louis-Alexandre Berthier, Prince de Wagram
- ☐ d. Laurent de Gouvion Saint-Cyr

10. Who did Napoleon appoint as his chief aide-de-camp upon taking command of the Army of Italy?

☐ a. Michel Ney

☐ b. Nicolas-Jean de Dieu Soult

☐ c. Louis Davout

☐ d. Joachim Murat

"Radio the ole man we'll be late on account of a thousand mile detour."

GENERAL, MULTIPLE CHOICE

1. Which castle was the last stronghold of the Hojo clan before it fell in 1590?

   ☐ a. Akashi   ☐ b. Edo
   ☐ c. Odawara   ☐ d. Itami

2. Which military theorist coined the term "fog of war"?

   ☐ a. Chevalier Folard   ☐ b. Carl von Clausewitz
   ☐ c. Niccoló Machiavelli   ☐ d. Napoleon Bonaparte

3. Which Duke of Burgundy captured Paris in 1418?

   ☐ a. Philip the Bold   ☐ b. Charles the Bold
   ☐ c. Philip the Good   ☐ d. John the Fearless

4. The "Battle above the Clouds" occurred during which American Civil War campaign?

   ☐ a. Chickamauga   ☐ b. Chattanooga
   ☐ c. Vicksburg   ☐ d. Fredericksburg

5. Which king led the Scots to victory at the 1010 battle of Mortlack?

   ☐ a. Kenneth III   ☐ b. Duncan I
   ☐ c. Malcolm II   ☐ d. Macbeth

Although I cannot ensure success, I will endeavour to deserve it.
Admiral John Paul Jones

6. In which year was the last Grand Master of the Knights Templar burned for heresy?

    ❑ a. 1314   ❑ b. 1337
    ❑ c. 1349   ❑ d. 1365

7. "Skanderbeg" or George Kastioti is a war hero of which country?

    ❑ a. Albania   ❑ b. Hungary
    ❑ c. Romania   ❑ d. Bulgaria

8. Which battle, fought in 1213, saw the death of Pedro II of Aragon and the effective end of the Albigensian cause?

    ❑ a. Bouvines   ❑ b. Muret
    ❑ c. Damme   ❑ d. Fornham

9. Who did Gustavus Adolphus marry in 1620?

    ❑ a. Princes Maria Elizabeth
    ❑ b. Christina of Holstein-Gottorp
    ❑ c. Duchess Anna of Prussia
    ❑ d. Maria Eleanora of Brandenburg

10. In which engagement did King Harald Hardrada defeat the fleet of Sweyn II of Denmark?

    ❑ a. Kinlos   ❑ b. Bornhöved
    ❑ c. Nissa   ❑ d. Mortlack

QUIZ 95
GENERAL, SHORT ANSWER

1. Which mercenary led the "Ye Ancient Order of Frothblowers"?

. . . .

2. What was the first ship to launch an airplane from its decks?

. . . .

3. Who was the highest-ranking American officer to be killed during World War II?

. . . .

4. Who led the 1212 Children's Crusade?

. . . .

5. Who was the first female tank crewman to be named a Hero of the Soviet Union?

. . . .

6. Upon landing in Egypt in 1798, did Napoleon's Army of the Orient have more than 4,000 cavalry, or less?

. . . .

Pity the warrior who is contented to crawl about in the beggardom of rules! ... What genius does must be the best of rules, and theory cannot do better than to show how and why it is so.

Carl von Clausewitz

DID YOU KNOW?

Peter Francisco, the "Virginia Giant," was arguably one of the greatest soldiers in American history. An orphan found wandering the Virginia docks in 1765, he would later join the American Revolution fighting under George Washington in many of the biggest battles of the war. Too large to wield a normal sword, Washington had a special 5ft blade made for him. His greatest feat came at the retreat from Camden, when he pulled a 1,000lb cannon free of its gun carriage and carried it to safety.

7. Which Duke of Apulia had a wife named Sicelgaeta who often accompanied her husband into battle dressed in full armor?

. . . .

8. The crusader, Jean Le Meingre "Boucicaut," was a member of which chivalric order?

. . . .

9. In modern US military terminology, what is a "boomerang"?

. . . .

10. During World War II, what was the numerical designation of the "Americal Division"?

. . . .

QUIZ 96
WAR IN CHINA, MULTIPLE CHOICE

1. Which Chinese warlord was known as the "Dog Meat General"?

   ❑ a. Chang Tsung-ch'ang   ❑ b. Tsa Ting-kai
   ❑ c. Chang Hsueh-liang   ❑ d. Jen Yuan-tao

2. Which American officer was appointed as chief of staff to Chiang Kai-shek in 1942?

   ❑ a. Lewis Pick   ❑ b. Joseph Stilwell
   ❑ c. Daniel Sultan   ❑ a. Albert Wedermeyer

3. In which year was the Chinese Communist Party established?

   ❑ a. 1916   ❑ b. 1918
   ❑ c. 1921   ❑ d. 1924

4. Which Chinese military scholar wrote *The Biographies of One Hundred Generals*?

   ❑ a. Sun Tzu   ❑ b. Tu Mu
   ❑ c. Mei Yao-ch'en   ❑ d. Chang Yu

5. Which king established the permanent Shang capital at Yin around 1300 BC?

   ❑ a. Shou Hsin   ❑ b. Pan-k'eng
   ❑ c. Yao   ❑ d. Wu Ting

6. A military official of the 5th grade under the Ming dynasty was identified by which animal depicted on embroidered patches on his outfit?

☐ a. Lion   ☐ b. Tiger
☐ c. Leopard   ☐ d. Bear

7. Ch'i Chi-kuang's "Mandarin duck" formations contained how many men?

☐ a. 4   ☐ b. 12
☐ c. 20   ☐ d. 50

8. The Righteous Harmonious Fists, or Boxer Society, was officially abolished with the passing of the "Boxer Protocol" on which date?

☐ a. December 22, 1900   ☐ b. January 1, 1901
☐ c. September 7, 1901   ☐ d. July 24, 1906

9. Frederick Ward's Ever-Victorious Army was founded and fought in which war?

☐ a. 1st Opium War   ☐ b. 2nd Opium War
☐ c. Taiping Rebellion   ☐ d. Boxer Rebellion

10. Which "general" led the first Chinese troops into Korea in October 1950?

☐ a. P'eng Teh-huai   ☐ b. Wei Li-Huang
☐ c. Liao Yao-hsiang   ☐ d. Tu Yu-ming

DIFFICULT

GENERAL, MULTIPLE CHOICE

1. How many US Medals of Honor were awarded for actions in Somalia?

   ☐ a. 0   ☐ b. 1
   ☐ c. 2   ☐ d. 3

2. Which Ottoman sultan was known as "The Conqueror"?

   ☐ a. Murad II   ☐ b. Mehmet I
   ☐ c. Bayezid I   ☐ d. Mehmet II

3. Which nickname is often applied to the 1914 battle of Halen?

   ☐ a. Battle of the Cross Roads
   ☐ b. Battle of the Night Stars
   ☐ c. Battle of the Broken Blades
   ☐ d. Battle of the Silver Helmets

4. Which queen led the Burgundians to victory over the Neustrians at the 604 battle of Etampes?

   ☐ a. Ostrogotha   ☐ b. Brunehilde
   ☐ c. Dietlind   ☐ d. Grimhild

5. How many Turkish frigates were destroyed during the Russian attack on Sinope in 1853?

   ☐ a. 0   ☐ b. 1
   ☐ c. 7   ☐ d. 18

6. Which battle, fought in 1644, saw the Marquis of Montrose defeat Covenanters under Lord Elcho despite being heavily outnumbered?

☐ a. Tippermuir   ☐ b. Cropredy Bridge
☐ c. Auldern   ☐ d. Aberdeen

7. Which British general wrote a play called *The Maid of Seven Oaks*?

☐ a. George Augustus Howe
☐ b. John Churchill, Duke of Marlborough
☐ c. Colin Campbell
☐ d. John Burgoyne

8. The original "Dog Soldiers" belonged to which Native American tribe?

☐ a. Cherokee   ☐ b. Crow
☐ c. Cheyenne   ☐ d. Apache

9. Which date in 1927 saw the Nanchang Uprising, generally thought to mark the beginning of the Chinese Civil War?

☐ a. January 13   ☐ b. March 27
☐ c. August 1   ☐ d. November 11

10. Who did János Hunyadi support in the 1439 civil war in the Holy Roman Empire?

☐ a. Sigismund of Luxemburg
☐ b. Albert I
☐ c. Wladislaw III
☐ d. László V of Bohemia

DIFFICULT

MILITARY ANAGRAMS

Unscramble the famous war, battle, movie, author, etc...

1. Queen torn after hot till news (3, 5, 2, 3, 7, 5)

. . . .

2. Pet story fable (6, 2, 5)

. . . .

© Stars & Stripes

"You gents relax. We got six inches of armor."

3. Man aircrew (7, 3)

. . . .

4. Open apron on a table (8, 9)

. . . .

5. As he lends pace (13)

. . . .

6. A plot on (7)

. . . .

7. Etch geese apart (3, 5, 6)

. . . .

8. Karate hen row (3, 6, 3)

. . . .

9. Fat worms espoused sanction (7, 2, 4, 11)

. . . .

10. Lincoln with crush (7, 9)

. . . .

11. Narrative's navy pig (6, 7, 4)

. . . .

12. Ignoble ship syrup (6, 10)

. . . .

13. Ask Mango Nuts (5, 7)

. . . .

14. Entered her hut (3, 4, 6)

. . . .

ANSWERS

QUIZ 64 THE EASTERN FRONT
1)d 2)a 3)d 4)c 5)a 6)c 7)b 8)d 9)b 10)c

QUIZ 65 GENERAL
1)d 2)a 3)b 4)c 5)b 6)c 7)b 8)a 9)d 10)a

QUIZ 66 GENERAL
1) John Pope
2) Pius VI
3) Four
4) Admiral Maarten Tromp
5) Ephialtes of Trachis
6) L'Entreprenant "The Enterprising," which made its debut at the battle of Fleurus in 1794
7) Aachen
8) Hasdrubal and Mago
9) Three – Australia, New Zealand, and the United States
10) The Seven Weeks' War (or Austro–Prussian War)

QUIZ 67 NATIVE AMERICAN WARS
1)d 2)a 3)b 4)b 5)c 6)d 7)b 8)b 9)a 10)d

QUIZ 68 GENERAL
1)c 2)d 3)a 4)c 5)a 6)b 7)d 8)b 9)a 10)b

QUIZ 69 GENERAL
1) False. The Pacification of Berwick ended the First Bishops' War in 1639
2) True
3) True
4) False. She was sentenced to 10–30 years and served less than 12 years
5) False. One man is known to have accomplished this feat, Franz von Werra
6) True
7) False. It was a Gardner gun that jammed. Kipling misidentifies it in his famous poem
8) True. (October 4, 1943; June 24, 1946; June 7, 1952)
9) True, along with five other leaders of the fleet
10) True

QUIZ 70 HORATIO NELSON
1)d 2)d 3)a 4)b 5)c 6)a 7)d 8)b 9)d 10)b

QUIZ 71 GENERAL
1)d 2)a 3)c 4)d 5)d 6)b 7)a 8)d 9)a 10)b

QUIZ 72 GENERAL
1) Znaim. Zürich will also be accepted
2) Vigo Bay
3) 155mm M1
4) Robert Baden-Powell
5) The atomic bombing of Nagasaki
6) Stanislas Leszczynski
7) Snider rifle
8) Regenbogen (rainbow)
9) The British
10) Operation *Bricklayer*

QUIZ 73 RUSSIAN AND SOVIET COMMANDERS
1)d 2)b 3)d 4)a 5)b 6)b 7)d 8)a 9)b 10)d

QUIZ 74 GENERAL
1)c 2)a 3)b 4)c 5)d 6)a 7)a 8)c 9)d 10)c

QUIZ 75 GENERAL
1) True. Finland was part of Russia at the time
2) True
3) False
4) True – in 1830
5) True. It was employed in the Second Battle of Breitenfeld in 1642
6) False. That honor belongs to the "American Turtle" during the American Revolution
7) False
8) True
9) True – in 1956
10) False. It has never launched any

QUIZ 76 THE THIRTY YEARS' WAR
1)b 2)a 3)c 4)a 5)b 6)d 7)a 8)b 9)c 10)d

QUIZ 77 GENERAL
1)d 2)c 3)b 4)d 5)d 6)d 7)b 8)a 9)b 10)d

QUIZ 78 GENERAL
1) Mohammed Saeed Al-Sahaf, better known as "Comical Ali," the Iraqi Information Minister

2) Sino–Japanese War of 1937 (or Second Sino–Japanese War)
3) Horatio Nelson
4) Alcolea
5) George Sackville (or George Germain)
6) Paul von Lettow-Vorbeck
7) The Swiss
8) Akechi Mitsuhide
9) James FitzJames, Duke of Berwick
10) Winfield Scott

QUIZ 79 WORLD WAR II IN ITALY
1)c 2)c 3)d 4)d 5)b 6)d 7)b 8)d 9)c 10)b

QUIZ 80 GENERAL
1)c 2)c 3)c 4)c 5)a 6)c 7)b 8)b 9)d 10)d

QUIZ 81 GENERAL
1) False
2) False. Although Foch was in the army, he saw no active service during the Franco-Prussian War
3) True
4) True
5) True, according to legend anyway…
6) False. Former Vice-President John Breckinridge served as a Confederate general and fought in several battles
7) False. He came fifth in the modern pentathlon in the 1912 Olympics
8) True. Their last recorded use is in 1629 at the battle of Honigfeld
9) True. It goes back to at least the American Civil War and possibly the Mexican–American War
10) True

QUIZ 82 THE VIETNAM WAR
1)b 2)a 3)b 4)b 5)b 6)d 7)d 8)c 9)d 10)c

QUIZ 83 GENERAL
1)c 2)b 3)c 4)b 5)d 6)b 7)d 8)a 9)a 10)a

QUIZ 84 GENERAL
1) George H. W. Bush
2) André Masséna
3) The Danes
4) Sir Thomas Fairfax
5) A Ninja, or a "person of stealth"

6) Trick question – it is not known how the Romans saluted, or even if they did so
7) Cerignola in 1503
8) David Marshall "Carbine" Williams
9) "…dear friends, once more," from Shakespeare's *Henry V*
10) Jean Baptiste Vaquette de Gribeauval

QUIZ 85 THE WAR FOR IRELAND
1)a 2)a 3)b 4)d 5)b 6)d 7)a 8)b 9)b 10)d

QUIZ 86 GENERAL
1)a 2)c 3)d 4)c 5)d 6)b 7)a 8)b 9)d 10)a

QUIZ 87 GENERAL
1) False. He never applied. He was turned down by the Naval Academy
2) False. He died after falling from his horse in 1868
3) False. The term predates the conflict by at least 100 years
4) True. 7,000 soldiers participated and over 8,000 medals were awarded
5) True, officially
6) True
7) True
8) True. Guilford Courthouse, Hobkirk's Hill, Fort Ninety-six, and Eutaw Springs
9) False. "Genocide" as a crime did not exist until after the trials
10) True, in 1906

QUIZ 88 GENERAL
1)d 2)b 3)d 4)c 5)b 6)c 7)c 8)a 9)c 10)c

QUIZ 89 GENERAL
1) HMS *Severn* and HMS *Mersey*
2) Ludwig Beck
3) Philip Henry Sheridan
4) Ivan Stepanovich Konev
5) Lennart Torstensson, Count of Ortala
6) Major General "Mad Anthony" Wayne
7) Sir Edmund Verney
8) The Treaty of Tartu
9) Jean Baptist, Count d'Arco
10) Stilwell

QUIZ 90 DIXIE
1)d 2)c 3)b 4)d 5)a 6)d 7)b 8)a 9)b 10)c

QUIZ 91 GENERAL
1)d 2)d 3)d 4)c 5)b 6)c 7)c 8)c 9)d 10)a

QUIZ 92 GENERAL
1) True. In the battle of the Yellow Sea between Korea and Japan, the Koreans under Admiral Yi Sung Sin had two ironclad ships
2) False. That honor goes to the Polish volunteer Anderzej Tadeusz Bonawentura Kosciuszko
3) False. He spent about one year as a slave on a Turkish galley
4) True, technically. All production after February 1942 was claimed by the military
5) True
6) True
7) False. The vast majority were Irish
8) False. He did go to America, but arrived too late to see any action
9) True. In fact the number is closer to 4,000
10) True

QUIZ 93 NAPOLEON'S MARSHALS
1)c 2)a 3)d 4)c 5)c 6)c 7)b 8)a 9)a 10)d

QUIZ 94 GENERAL
1)c 2)a 3)d 4)b 5)c 6)a 7)a 8)b 9)d 10)c

QUIZ 95 GENERAL
1) "Mad" Mike Hoare
2) USS *Birmingham*, on November 14, 1910
3) Lieutenant General Lesley McNair (will also accept Frank Maxwell Andrews and Simon Bolivar Buckner, Jr)
4) Stephen of Cloyes (will also accept Nicholas of Germany)
5) Mariya Oktyabrskaya
6) Less
7) Robert Guiscard
8) *Emprised l'Escu verta a la Dame Blanche* (Enterprise of the green shield with the White Lady)
9) A device used for locating enemy snipers
10) It had none, but was later designated the 23rd Division

QUIZ 96 WAR IN CHINA
1)a 2)b 3)c 4)d 5)b 6)d 7)b 8)c 9)c 10)a

QUIZ 97 GENERAL
1)c 2)d 3)d 4)b 5)c 6)a 7)d 8)c 9)c 10)c

QUIZ 98 MILITARY ANAGRAMS

1) *All Quiet on the Western Front*
2) Battle of Ypres
3) Crimean War
4) Napoleon Bonaparte
5) Passchendaele
6) *Platoon*
7) *The Great Escape*
8) The Korean War
9) Weapons of Mass Destruction
10) Winston Churchill
11) *Saving Private Ryan*
12) Osprey Publishing
13) Angus Konstam
14) *The Deer Hunter*

DIFFICULT

FOUR-STAR GENERAL
KNOWLEDGE

GENERAL, MULTIPLE CHOICE

1. Which Vietnamese hero launched a surprise attack on the Tet holiday in 1789 that drove the Chinese out of Vietnam?

   ❏ a. Dai Vet   ❏ b. Nguyen Hue
   ❏ c. Boa Dai   ❏ d. Nguyen Ahn

2. Which of the following is NOT a nickname applied to US Marine Major General Smedley Darlington Butler?

   ❏ a. Old Gimlet Eye   ❏ b. Old Duckboard
   ❏ c. The Fighting Quaker   ❏ d. Old Boatrock

3. Which Peruvian leader led his forces to victory at the 1532 battle of Ambate?

   ❏ a. Atahualpa   ❏ b. Huascar
   ❏ c. Almagro   ❏ d. Huaman

4. Which of the following was NOT one of Chief Joseph's war leaders during the 1877 Nez Percé War?

   ❏ a. Rainbow   ❏ b. Looking Glass
   ❏ c. Five Wounds   ❏ d. Silver Star

The regular officer has the traditions of 40 generations of serving soldiers behind him, and to him the old weapons are the most honored.

T. E. Lawrence

5. Who led the Serbians during the 1885 battle of Slivnica?

☐ a. Prince Alexander ☐ b. King Milan IV
☐ c. King Petar I ☐ d. King Ivan II

6. Colin Campbell, Baron Clyde, was born with what surname?

☐ a. McCulloch ☐ b. Macliver
☐ c. MacIver ☐ d. McCormack

7. What was the numerical designation of the regiment that later became "Prince Albert's Own Hussars"?

☐ a. 6th ☐ b. 9th
☐ c. 11th ☐ d. 13th

8. How many horses did Condé have shot out from under him during the 1674 battle of Senef?

☐ a. 2 ☐ b. 3
☐ c. 4 ☐ d. 5

9. Which World War II Japanese general conceived the incendiary balloon offensive against the United States?

☐ a. Sueyoshi Kusaba ☐ b. Harayuma Endo
☐ c. Mutsumikichi Ryuko ☐ d. Juro Adachi

10. On which date was Operation *Iraqi Freedom* launched?

☐ a. March 20, 2003 ☐ b. April 16, 2003
☐ c. May 1, 2003 ☐ d. May 30, 2003

QUIZ 100
GENERAL, MULTIPLE CHOICE

1. Which admiral led Task Force 11, which included the aircraft carrier USS *Lexington*, at the battle of the Coral Sea?

   ❑ a. Jack Frank   ❑ b. Aubrey Fitch
   ❑ c. John Crace   ❑ d. William Halsey

2. Which battle against the Arabs forced Byzantine Emperor Justinian II to agree to joint control of Cyprus?

   ❑ a. Syllaeum   ❑ b. Sebastopolis
   ❑ c. Cyzicus   ❑ d. Germanicopolis

3. Which country is credited with inventing the concept of the "trunnion" for artillery pieces?

   ❑ a. England   ❑ b. France
   ❑ c. Switzerland   ❑ d. Germany

4. The 1142 battle of the Iron Gates was fought near which river?

   ❑ a. Ebro   ❑ b. Danube
   ❑ c. Rhine   ❑ d. Po

5. In 1775, a group of American lumbermen led by Jeremiah O'Brien seized which British armed cutter?

   ❑ a. *Margaretta*   ❑ b. *Dolphin*
   ❑ c. *Swan*   ❑ d. *Queen Bess*

6. Which 955 battle saw the end of major Magyar military attacks into Germany?

☐ a. Riade
☐ b. Mersberg
☐ c. Drava
☐ d. Lechfeld

7. What is the oldest commissioned ship in the Chilean Navy?

☐ a. *Covadona*
☐ b. *Indepencia*
☐ c. *Esmeralda*
☐ d. *Huáscar*

8. Who established the first modern military academy in 1617?

☐ a. John of Nassau
☐ b. Gustavus Adolphus
☐ c. François-Michel le Tellier, Marquis de Louvois
☐ d. Lennart Torstensson

9. During the 1637–38 Shimabara Revolt, the rebels made their stand in which ancient fortress?

☐ a. Hara
☐ b. Osaka
☐ c. Hirado
☐ d. Nagasaki

10. The fortress of "A Famosa" is located in which country?

☐ a. Laos
☐ b. Malaysia
☐ c. Thailand
☐ d. Vietnam

Terrain for the military man is much the same as the chess board for the player who wants to move his pawns, knights and elephants in the most effective way.

Frederick the Great

QUIZ 101
GENERAL, MULTIPLE CHOICE

1. Which Native American tribe allied with the Dutch settlers during the 1641–45 Algonquin War?

   ❑ a. Mohawk ❑ b. Abenaki
   ❑ c. Mohican ❑ d. Hurons

2. Who commanded the Japanese Fourteenth Army during their 1941 invasion of the Philippines?

   ❑ a. Shojiro Iida ❑ b. Tomitoro Horii
   ❑ c. Masaharu Homma ❑ d. Takeo Takagi

3. Which of the following UN member states did NOT contribute ground troops to the Korean War?

   ❑ a. Luxembourg ❑ b. Columbia
   ❑ c. Ethiopia ❑ d. India

4. In what year was the Antarctic Treaty signed?

   ❑ a. 1959 ❑ b. 1965
   ❑ c. 1971 ❑ d. 1977

5. Which submarine accomplished the first underwater circumnavigation of the world?

   ❑ a. USS *Nautilus* ❑ b. USS *George Washington*
   ❑ c. USS *Triton* ❑ d. USS *Ethan Allen*

6. How many British regiments received battle honors during the American Revolution?

   ❑ a. 26   ❑ b. 21
   ❑ c. 18   ❑ d. 0

7. Mangal Pandey, one of the figureheads of the 1857 Indian Mutiny, was a sepoy in which regiment?

   ❑ a. 34th Bengal Native Infantry
   ❑ b. 2nd Bengal Light Cavalry
   ❑ c. the Sirmoor Rifle Regiment
   ❑ d. 1st Bengal Military Police

8. The 1948 Karen Revolt occurred in which country?

   ❑ a. Thailand   ❑ b. Burma
   ❑ c. Nepal   ❑ d. Pakistan

9. Which special forces unit originally trained in the camps of *El Infierno* (Hell) and *La Pólvora* (Gunpowder)?

   ❑ a. Guatemala's *Kaibiles*
   ❑ b. Mexico's *Grupo Aeromóvil de Fuerzas Especiales*
   ❑ c. Spain's *Unidad de Operaciones Especiales*
   ❑ d. Brazil's *Batalhão de Operaçoes Policias Especiais*

10. In which year during the Seminole Wars did the Dade Massacre occur?

   ❑ a. 1818   ❑ b. 1824
   ❑ c. 1829   ❑ d. 1835

IMPOSSIBLE

GENERAL, MULTIPLE CHOICE

1. Which of the following was NOT a gun cast by the Russian Andrey Chokhov?

   ❑ a. Unicorn   ❑ b. Vixen
   ❑ c. Wolf   ❑ d. Witch

2. How many fingers did Banastre Tarelton lose during the 1781 battle of Guilford Courthouse?

   ❑ a. 1   ❑ b. 2
   ❑ c. 3   ❑ d. 5

3. The 1813 Treaty of Gulistan ended which conflict?

   ❑ a. the Russo-Turkish War   ❑ b. the Polish Insurrection
   ❑ c. the Russo-Persian War   ❑ d. the Turko-Egyptian War

4. Who funded the film *The Life of General Villa*?

   ❑ a. Pancho Villa   ❑ b. Mutual Film Corporation
   ❑ c. Victoriano Huerta   ❑ d. the US government

To give reputation to the army of any state, it is necessary to revive the discipline of the ancients, cherish it and honor it, and give it life, so that in return it may give reputation to the state.
Niccolo Machiavelli

5. Who led the New South Wales officers who arrested Captain William Bligh during the 1806 Rum Rebellion?

- ☐ a. George Johnston
- ☐ b. Talford Smith
- ☐ c. Joseph Bollin
- ☐ d. Henry Christopher

6. Who commanded the Spanish squadron as it entered the 1898 battle of Manila Bay?

- ☐ a. Pacual Cavera y Topete
- ☐ b. Patrico Montojo
- ☐ c. Manuel Macías y Casado
- ☐ d. Romón Blanco y Erenas

7. Which of these battles of the War of the Triple Alliance occurred last chronologically?

- ☐ a. Paso de Patria
- ☐ b. Uruguayana
- ☐ c. Curupayty
- ☐ d. Ypacarai

8. What was the original name of the regiment later renamed "97th Queen's Own German Regiment"?

- ☐ a. Minorca Regiment
- ☐ b. Piedmontese Leigon
- ☐ c. Roll's Regiment
- ☐ d. Meuron Regiment

9. Which Japanese general officially surrendered the Japanese armed forces on the deck of the USS *Missouri* in 1945?

- ☐ a. Hjime Sugiyama
- ☐ b. Yoshijiro Umezu
- ☐ c. Kuniaki Koiso
- ☐ d. Kideki Tojo

10. How many rowers were normally employed on a Viking *fimtansessa* longship?

- ☐ a. 26
- ☐ b. 30
- ☐ c. 36
- ☐ d. 44

GENERAL, MULTIPLE CHOICE

1. Whose land sale instigated the First Taranaki War?

   ❑ a. Wiremu Kingi
   ❑ b. Pokikake Te Teira
   ❑ c. Te Kooti Arikirangi Te Turuki
   ❑ d. Riwha Titokowaru

2. Helmuth Karl Bernhard, later Graf von Moltke, began his military service with which nation?

   ❑ a. Prussia   ❑ b. Austria
   ❑ c. Hungary   ❑ d. Denmark

3. Which of these was the highest rank?

   ❑ a. *Feldwebel*   ❑ b. *Obrist*
   ❑ c. *Locotenent*   ❑ d. *Gemeinweibel*

4. How many servicemen were awarded the Knight's Cross with Diamonds during World War II?

   ❑ a. 12   ❑ b. 16
   ❑ c. 22   ❑ d. 27

If ever there is another war in Europe, it will come out of some damned silly thing in the Balkans.

Otto von Bismarck

5. In the Aztec military, which title meant "chief of the house of javelins"?

   ❑ a. tlacatacatl   ❑ b. tlacateca-techtli
   ❑ c. tlacochcalcatl   ❑ d. ichcahuipilli

6. Which was the only British line regiment to contribute multiple company-sized detachments to the 1870 Red River Campaign in Canada?

   ❑ a. 42nd   ❑ b. 60th
   ❑ c. 68th   ❑ d. 72nd

7. Which Native American tribe sided against the North Carolina colonists in the Tuscarora War?

   ❑ a. Yamasee   ❑ b. Apalachee
   ❑ c. Coree   ❑ d. Cherokee

8. What was the first breech-loading firearm officially adopted for service in the French Army?

   ❑ a. Chassepot   ❑ b. Fusil Lance
   ❑ c. Dresye needle-gun   ❑ d. Reffye Mitrailleuse

9. How many times was Eric Hartman shot down (or forced to crash-land) during World War II?

   ❑ a. 0   ❑ b. 4
   ❑ c. 8   ❑ d. 16

10. Confederate guerrilla John Singleton Mosby later served as the US consul in which city?

   ❑ a. Beijing   ❑ b. Hong Kong
   ❑ c. Istanbul   ❑ d. Sydney

ANSWERS

QUIZ 99 GENERAL
1)b 2)d 3)a 4)d 5)b 6)b 7)c 8)b 9)a 10)a

QUIZ 100 GENERAL
1)b 2)b 3)b 4)b 5)a 6)d 7)d 8)a 9)a 10)b

QUIZ 101 GENERAL
1)a 2)c 3)d 4)a 5)c 6)d 7)a 8)b 9)a 10)d

QUIZ 102 GENERAL
1)d 2)b 3)c 4)b 5)a 6)b 7)d 8)a 9)b 10)b

QUIZ 103 GENERAL
1)b 2)d 3)b 4)d 5)c 6)c 7)c 8)b 9)d 10)b

ACKNOWLEDGEMENTS

The Osprey Quizmaster would like to thank Phil Smith for his help in gathering, clarifying and standardizing, and the Osprey Quiz Team for their work checking facts and challenging conceptions.

THE OSPREY QUIZ TEAM
Etienne Huygens
Theo van Deelen
Alexandre Machado
David Casserly
Timmy De Cabooter
Graham Travers
Juan A. Rivera
Krister Fritzon
David Logan
Jonathan Walters
Stuart Johnston
Phil Peterson
Andrew Banks